Kim,

Thank you Greatly for your support & Helping Me to Help our Youth's

God Bless's

Success is Not about what you can Do, but yet,

It's About What You Can *Endure...*

- Sean Ingram

SEAN INGRAM INTERNATIONAL
AFRICA - ASIA — EUROPE — THE AMERICAS

This book is the autobiographical accounts of Sean Ingram's journey in life from poverty to prison to prosperity.

No parts of this book may be reproduced, electrical or otherwise for any reason without Authors written consent.

Published by:
Sean Ingram & Company
email@seaningram.info
www.SeanIngram.info

Copyright © 2017 by Sean Ingram

Cover Design by Sean Ingram
Cover Photography by Chris Charles
www.CreativeSilence.net

Library of Congress
ISBN: 978-0-9749049-6-2
Printed in the United States of America

In this book it is my desire to inspire, encourage, motivate and be an example for you that dreams can and do come true. Within my transparency, I pray that you will see yourself.

This book is dedicated to the youth. I have shared with you the trials of my testimony and the many lessons that I have learned in my life from every situation that I have had to persevere in my process during my journey from poverty to prison to prosperity.

I will share all of me with you, but if you remember nothing else from the lessons of stories within this book, please do remember these three things, which is truly the secret to my success.

I BELIEVE IN GOD

I BELIEVE IN SEAN INGRAM

I BELIEVE IN THE TALENTS
GOD HAS GIVEN SEAN INGRAM TO SUCCEEED

Author & Motivational Speaker

Contents

In Memory of...

My Lord Jesus who died for me. My Grandmother Retha Mae Hagans who lived for me. My Grandfather Leroy Lewis who raised me to stand as a man. My Mother Delores Franklin who passed down the gift of writing and creativity to me. My Uncles Phillip and Joe Ingram who guided, protected and educated me on the lows of life. My God Brother Kendrick Best who looked up to me. My dearest childhood friends David Sherrod and JJ Thompson who left me way to soon, thanks for sharing with me your gifts and dreams, I promise you both to keep them alive.

I also dedicate this book to all of my other family, friends and fans whom have died along the journey.

Introduction

Fifty-four months and a wake-up, the thought resonated in my mind with endless echoes as an old broken record. My eyes opened to a scripted collage of chaotic harmony and prayers, obscenities and gang feuds intertwined though tributes written beneath the overhead bunk bed. My nightmare was now becoming a reality to me. I looked over to my right, then my left, but in all directions, my reality stayed the same. Later I learned that due to complications with my paperwork during the process of my transition from county jail to home confinement to me self surrendering to federal prison, somewhere in the transition, my paperwork became misplaced, therefore I would have to stay in solitary confinement before entering into population. A month later, I was finally moved onto the yard and into the Wake B dormitory, where I would spend a little over the next four years of my life.

During my time in solitary confinement, I conversed with myself daily; actually, most often I envisioned roundtable conversations between myself, God and Satan. I sat quietly listening to the debates of negotiations over my life between God and Satan. Though I never said a word within the conversations, I knew I had a choice to make. My choices were simple, either A, keep running with Satan and continue to advocate for the negativity and wrong which I had risked my life for so many times before that would inevitably promise me life in prison or death, or either B, change directions in this fork in the road I've found myself standing in front of and begin to go in the direction in which I truly believed that God had destined for me, the road that would ultimately lead me to the promise land which I have been so desperately searching for my entire life.

I truly felt and believed in my heart that it was time for me to stop straddling the fence, but I was afraid that the grass wouldn't be greener on the other side of the fence than from the side I felt so familiar and comfortable with. I looked beneath my feet only to realize that the green grass I stood on for many years was already dead. The fence began to grow higher and higher, swathing with barbwire at its top with every breath I took. It was obvious that I had no choice but to change sides if I indeed wanted to live a life of prosperity and not of struggling and suffering.

Night and day, silently I had private conversations with God. I questioned him, interrogated him, doubted him and even trusted him.

I inquired of God, "What Do You Want of Me?"

His reply pierced my soul. The clarity of the vision he showed me amazed and scared me simultaneously.

Silently his voice said to me, "I have given you a great gift that you have often used to glorify Satan rather than me. I have allowed you to live and learn from the many mistakes that you have made. I have allowed you to persevere all of the heartache and pain, trials and tribulations, feelings of depression, loneliness and suicide. I have ordered your steps to lead you to this very moment. I have tested you in order to give you your testimony so that you will give life through your words to those who are despondent and dying inside of their living corpse. I have strengthened you and made you fearless in the face of those who will oppose you. I have chosen you to share my message. Use the gifts and talents in which I have given unto you for me, and the building of my kingdom. That is all that I ask of you."

The scripture, to whom much is given, much is required, scrolled through my mind. My choice was made. I didn't know what or how, I just knew it was to be. I prayed, I listened, I waited, I dreamed. I knew that change had to start within, wasn't sure if it was to be first in my heart or first in my mind, but I knew eventually, both had to be renewed. I continued to Pray, Listen, Wait and Dream. Each day, in the oddest way, a revelation would be revealed to me sometimes though conversations with other inmates and at times from correction officers, but most often through my many thoughts and dreams.

It came to my realization that I had to first change my mindset, and then all else would follow. Although true that the mind or thought process can't control the heart's muscular functions within the circulatory system, but it does control the functions of thoughts and emotions. I dedicated myself to thinking differently about myself, my situation and my purpose and position in life. To encourage the change of my mindset, I began reading inspirational and motivational books, beginning with the Bible. I started monitoring the conversations I included myself into. I began to personally sensor the visuals I allowed myself to partake in, most influential, the magazines I read and television shows I would watch. I stayed mindful of the mindset of the people I would choose to associate myself with. I realized that in order for me to change my mindset, I had to change what I allowed to enter into my mind.

Twenty-three hours a day, I spent my time changing my mindset in order to better me. I came to grips with losing my mother only days before coming into prison. I had made peace with all of the confusion and anger I grew up with towards her, feeling that if she had made different choices for her life, then my life would have surely been different also. I forgave her, and prayed that she had forgiven me before she passed. I reflected on our relationship, the good and bad times, the ups and downs, her addictions, my choices, our mental and emotional issues and the gifts and talents that would connect us forever despite our apparent separation in life.

My mother was an artist also. She painted professionally mostly, but I later in life learned that she was also a writer in her early years. Though what I thought was separate lives, our story was indeed the same. Looking back, my gift for writing was subconsciously inspired by my mother from the beginning of my desire to write. Instead of despising my mother for, as I thought, her choosing her addictions and life style over me, I began to thank her for the gifts she passed down to me. I began to appreciate her for teaching me to nurture my gifts and talents, even when it seems it may be against all odds. She encouraged me to never give up on my dreams, as she had in life.

I reminisce on the morning my mother passed away. I remember vividly her calling me oddly at five o'clock in the morning. I answered, said hello, and listened to the silence being intermittently broken by breathing before her voice uttered.

Softly and sweetly she spoke, "I know that you are going through a lot right now, but I need you to stay and be strong for your little brother when I'm gone. Mommy's going home baby."

My mother had been diagnosed as a functional Schizophrenic from her many years of suffering with drug addiction and depression, so I listened in respect, thinking to myself that she was just going through one of her many and often hallucinogenic episodes. She gave me instructions for her funeral and informed me that what she wanted to wear would already be laid out on her bed. Months prior, she had my grandfather, her father, buy her a pre-paid burial package so all of the funeral arrangements would already be taken care of in order to save any stress or strain of burying her on my brother and me and the rest of the family.

She further inquired of my present situation with a joke, "I know you don't really want to go to prison, so would you rather go with me. I'm sure that heaven is a lot better place than prison."

I laughed at to what I thought was a joke, but later would learn that it would be her last words to me. I responded, "I will be alright, I'm not ready to die now, so I will take my chances in prison."

She laughed and told me that she loved me. She really wanted me to understand that despite our past, that she loved me with all of her heart. She asked for my forgiveness, I forgave her, and she then told me to hold on and be strong, go though the fire and pressure so that I can come out as a diamond.

She told me, "Goodbye", and I said, "Goodnight", even though it was already morning.

I awoke to the weeping of my grandmother. It was then I learned that my mothers phone call was much more than an episode, but actually a prophecy. My mother had been admitted into Cherry Mental Hospital early that same morning, as usual and routinely, they gave my mom a shot to subdue and calm her down, but that shot would be later determined as overdosed which sent my mother into cardiac arrest. Admitted into Wayne Memorial Hospital, my mother laid brain dead on life support. I quickly called my home confinement officer to inquire about being released on a pass to visit my mother, and unknowingly, I had already been approved a weekend pass.

I sat hand and with my little brother before our mother as the doctor performed his final test of mommas' responsiveness to being off life support. No response, therefore we had to make a decision to keep her on or take her off life support. It was no choice at all, momma had already told us both that she didn't want to be held on life support, she had rather go on home with God. We sat together, hand in hand with each other and her as she took her last breath.

Ironically, when she transcended, all of my anger towards her did also. I realized that life is to live and not to survive. I realized that we are all destined to die whenever our time is chosen, no amount of fear, anger, or confusion can bring me peace when my time comes.

As strange as it may sound, my mothers' death inspired me to live. Now I'm dying to live, rather than living to die.

"Within My

Temporary Failures

I Found

Everlasting Success"

Lesson

"Persevere your Process"

PERSEVERE
To persist in or remain constant to a purpose, idea, or task in the face of obstacles or discouragement.

PROCESS
A series of actions, changes, or functions that bring about an end, or result.

(Defined by The American Heritage Dictionary of the English Language)

If there is life, there is growth. If there is growth, then there has to be a process associated with the growing of. Even in death, there is a process of decomposition. In life, our process may vary depending on our race or where we are born, the financial and social status in which we are born in, the environment in which we grew up and the inherited circumstances in which we are forced to endure without choice.

In 1977, I was born African-American and poor. I was born into poverty down a dirt path behind a corn field and was forced to use an outhouse until I was around nine years of age, which was none of my choice, but yet the life that was innately chosen for me. Despite my situation and circumstance, I had to play the hand I was dealt in life because the only other option I had, or anyone has for that matter, is to give up and fold.

When we think of process, we think of the procedures, steps, activities and occurrences that happen in a person life in order for their progression. Unfortunately, every child isn't born in the most habitable living conditions conducive to proper growth in life. Similar to a seed being planted into rocky dry soil, which is definitely not the best conditions for this seed to have the opportunity to grow from beneath the ground, and be allowed the chance to reach its highest heights or fullest potential. Due to the state of the soil, it's more likely than not that the seed will surely die beneath the ground.

Imagine if you will, the seed in which we are speaking of are apple seeds. Imagine these apple seeds are the hope of a village of people, serving as their only source of food and finances. What choices do the farmers have, being that they had no choice of where they currently reside and the state of the soil in which their farm is made? Survival isn't an option, it's a must. The only option the farmer has is to cultivate the land until it's condition is good for the planting of the apple seeds. It will take many months or years of tilling, removing rocks and flipping over the soil to bring up the nutrient soil from deep below the ground. It wouldn't be an easy process, but it is possible to give life to a dying situation, and once you give life to the soil, then it's possible to bring life from out of that living soil.

I was born in rocky dry soil, or actually, I compare my life to the rose that grew through concrete. Despite the conditions I was born, I refused to die and not grow to reach my fullest potential.

Against all odds, I am determined to live. I am dedicated to succeeding. Though my process has been filled with tragedies and triumphs, trials and tribulations, I have endured and persevered every step of the way. The fire and pressure that I tolerated for many years of my life has turned me into the diamond that I am now. I started out as an unwanted piece of coal, but through time, fire and pressure, I have transformed into a diamond. Although transformed, my process isn't yet finished, now I have to continue my process of being cut, refined and polished in order for me to become valued as the value I know I have the potential to be.

It is all to common of the mentality of our youth, even many adults for that matter to desire relishing in the riches and fame of success but rather avoid the process of hard work and sacrifice that it takes to be successful. In my journey from poverty to prison to prosperity, I had to persevere many challenges that I honestly didn't know if I would make it through. More often than not, my greatest fear was that I would BREAKDOWN before I reached my BREAKTHROUGH.

Being successful is a triathlon race of discipline, determination, and endurance rather than a forty-yard dash of skill and talent.

The process will push you to your limit. The process will have you questioning yourself and your sanity. The process to success will serve as the TRUTH TEST that will determine if you are indeed deserving of the success you desire in your particular career choice.

How much are you willing to sacrifice? How hard are you willing to push yourself even when you feel like giving up? How dedicated are you, to you?

I remember many moments in my life and career that I had to push past fear, push past mental and emotional exhaustion and go even when I thought I couldn't go on.

I think about the times I traveled to perform or do book signings with only enough gas in the car to get me to the venue or bookstore. I had no choice but to go, even though I had no idea how I was going to get back, but at that moment, getting back was irrelevant because truly I couldn't afford to go, but I couldn't afford NOT to go even more. I remember vividly the many days and nights I stood alone outside in the cold and rain passing out flyers while fundraising at the fair ground flea market or Wal-Mart's. My grandma would always use to say that, "Sometimes you gotta go, even if you gotta go alone".

I found that statement to be more relevant to my life than I ever could have imagined when she said it.

I think about the time I was blessed with being awarded The International Merit of Poetry Award. I received the letter with so much excitement, but as I continued to read, my elation transformed into depression. I realized that the reception would be held during a conference in Washington, DC. The price of the conference was free to me because I was being awarded, not to mention that I was given a complimentary vendor table, but the problem I had was getting there and where would I stay even if I could get there. At this point in my life, I was beyond broke. I couldn't even afford gas to get to work, no less than going to Washington, DC from North Carolina. I couldn't even afford to go to a bookstore and buy my own book, so how could I possibly order books that I could sale at the conference.

I mentally gave up on the opportunity, but my heart wouldn't allow me to throw in the towel that easily. It was then that I learned that I had to *Stop Stressing and Start Strategizing.*

I knew that my check from my job at the time wouldn't be enough to get me to DC or allow me to order a few books I could sale to put gas in my truck for the ride back home. With every thought of why I knew I wasn't going to be able to go, the thought of the possibility of making it happen fought harder and harder to prevail.

I began strategizing. How, Who, Why and What was the questions I began to ask myself. I sat patiently and listened to the silence of my thoughts. With no answers surfacing, I began to get frustrated and lose hope. I became angry.

Spoken Word had become my outlet to express my emotions and release my frustrations. I showed up at a local open mic intending to release my wrath on stage that night. I shared my story with the audience before I performed a poem I had recently written about "My Dreamed Deferred". I spoke passionately from the depths of my heart and soul. I spoke as If was the last time I would ever speak again, because truthfully, in my mind, it would be.

A standing ovation erupted at the end of my performance, which to me wasn't a performance at all; it was just me crying out the only way I knew how, through my words on that stage. When I walked off the stage, people started offering me donations to help me get to DC. Within defeat, I found Victory.

I learned from that moment that we all need help in life, but most of us suffer because our pride won't allow us ask for help. From that moment, I learned how to **Stimulate my Support** with the gift that God had given me.

I had one month before the conference to raise enough money for gas and ordering books. The donations that I raised on that night, I ordered books with so I could have books to sale at the open mics, knowing that I could raise more money if I had books to sale also. With books in my book bag, I went to every open mic I could find. When it was time for the conference, I had my books, gas and enough money to even reserve a hotel room for one night, even though it was a three-day conference. I was praying that I would sale enough books on that first day to be able to get the hotel room for the last two days of the conference, but unfortunately that didn't happen, so I just slept in my truck the remainder of my time at the conference.

I parked in the back of the hotel and would walk from the convention center into the hotel with the others that was also attending the conference. When they would get on the elevators to go up to their rooms, I would go up on the elevator and then walk back down the stairs to go get in my truck for the night. I took the bottle waters they gave us at the conference to wash my face, brush my teeth and take the best birdbath I could within the 20 ounces of water I had.

Many have questioned me through the years, if my sacrifice of obtaining my award was worth it. My response will never waiver from the truth that it was worth it then and still now in the most valuable way. I think for me at that time, it truly wasn't so much about the award as it was for me earning and receiving the recognition and validation that I had worked so hard for in my writing career.

That award awarded me the validation and confidence that I could compete internationally as a writer. I needed proof that my dream could be real, and that was indeed my proof.

Learning to persevere my process also taught me about patience. Most of the time, the process to get from A to Z is a very long and drawn out series of events in order to reach the end result. Musicians learning to play an instrument for the first time most often want to pick up their instrument of choice and begin playing their favorite song instantly, just as I did when I began learning to play the piano. Pianist don't start out playing like Mozart and neither does painters first work of art sells like Van Gogh.

When most people look at the name and brand of Sean Ingram, I understand to many that it may seem as if I just popped out of nowhere or became an overnight success. Many look at my now, but only very few know of my before and the process I've persevered to reach this point in my life.

I will admit, often it angers me when people don't seem to recognize my process. It angers me when people ask for free books, or free workshops because in my mind it tells me that they don't recognize or respect my process. They see the finished product, but don't take into account the many days and months I sat down thinking, strategizing and writing the book or preparing for a speech. They don't equate my educational value or manual labor into the price of my products, mainly because they think it's something that I just do and it's easy for me, so I guess it should be free for them, which is furthest from the truth.

Life is a process. Learning is a process. Growth is a process. Success is a process of many combinations of processes.

Regardless of the many obstacles and detours you will encounter within your process, you must stay persistent to your purpose. You must stay encouraged in the midst of being discouraged. Stay constant on your course despite the detours you will have to take from finding yourself standing at a dead end.

Please Understand, many will doubt and discourage you. Many will advise you to travel a path that will carry you away from your destination. Many will call you crazy and speak against you because of their lack of understanding of your purpose, but that is all part of your process.

I learned to understand that God gave me the vision of my dreams and the passion of my purpose, and the visions he gave me isn't necessarily for others to see. Those closets to you may not even understand or believe in your struggle for success. People whom you have never met may be more instrumental in the progression of your process rather than those who you expected to receive support from.

During your process, stay focused on the finish line. Even though you can't see it, know that it's there. With every step, know that you are getting closer.

Every time you fall, get back up and continue moving forward.

Allow you to believe in you, even when others don't. Look back over your life at all of the hurdles you have already had to jump in life. Look back at how far away from the starting line you have come and say, "I did it and I will continue to do it until I reach victory".

Don't become distracted or discouraged at everybody else running past you in the race, because they have to run their race just as if you have to run yours. Stay FOCUSED and continue to Follow One Course Until Successful.

The greatest educators prepare us now for the future.   The greatest lessons in life are learned now but are understood in the latter.

If your goal is to be truly successful, you must invest all your time, energy, finances and faith now in order to receive your return on your investment in the future, but the only way you can accomplish this goal is to Persevere your Process.

"Stop Stressing
and Start Strategizing"

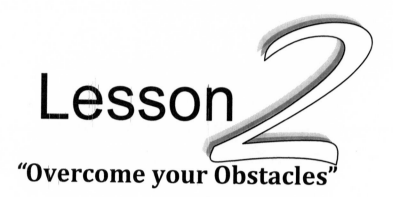

Lesson 2

"Overcome your Obstacles"

OVERCOME

To defeat in competition or conflict, conquer:

1. To prevail over:
2. To overpower, as with emotion; affect deeply.

OBSTACLE

One that opposes, stands in the way of, or holds up progress toward some goal.

(Defined by The American Heritage Dictionary of the English Language)

Most often, we stand from a distance looking at the mountain before us, doubting in wonderment, how will I ever reach my goal if I can't get over this mountain. The bewildering thoughts of How Can I, rather than, How Will I, seizes our determination. Without second thought, many will give up before they even begin the journey of overcoming their obstacles in life because of their fear of failure.

Fear of not succeeding often stems from the fear of unknowing, lack of preparation and not having the necessary tools needed to conquer your challenge that will allow you to overcome the particular obstacle that's presented before you. I've never climbed a mountain, but I can only imagine the amount of strength, endurance and knowledge that it will take to pull yourself up the steep, even if having the proper tools needed to assist in the mission.

I have grown to realize that obstacles are merely stepping stones in life in the form of mountains that stand before us, obstructing our path that leads us to our goals of success. For every obstacle that comes before us, we must know and truly believe that there is a way to overcome that obstacle if we indeed posses the will to do so.

Every day of my life, I proclaim, that this too shall past. I speak victory on conquering my challenges, in which I have accepted, that there will be many for me, and unfortunately not far few in between. Daily, weekly and monthly, I am ready and prepared to conquer the challenge of the new obstacles that I will have to overcome.

In my personal life, as well as business, I've had many obstacles to overcome, not to mention the many more that are just ahead patiently awaiting my arrival. Truth is, you have to be mentally and spiritually prepared in order to conquer many of the challenges that will challenge you. You will be tested like you have never been tested before. You will be afraid. You will become tired. You will want to give up. Your faith will be questioned. Your belief in yourself and God will become detained by doubt. In order for you to overcome some of the obstacles that you will face, you will be forced to dig deeper within yourself than you ever have before. You will be forced to believe like you have never believed before. You will fail over and over until you fail your way to success. You will be forced to be determined and dedicated to succeed like you never have before, because if not, failure will surely be your outcome.

Every obstacle you will face in life serves as a test for you. Ironically, the more test we take, the smarter we become. The harder we work to pass the test that is before us, the better chance we allow ourselves to get past the test and the more we equip ourselves with the necessary tools to help us pass and get past the next test that will surely come. I encourage you to Learn from your Lessons, so you can Learn your Lesson.

It is written that God will never give you more than you can bear, so it is a must that we keep the faith in believing that this obstacle we are being challenged to overcome, is only to build us up mentally and spiritually, and not to break us down. We must stay determined to reach our Breakthrough before our Breakdown.

When I left prison and entered into the halfway house, I was required to get a job. I didn't want just any job, but I wanted to work in the field of commercial refrigeration.

While incarcerated, I attended the HVAC program that was being offered at Butner FCI through Vance Granville Community College. After a conversation me and some of the other inmates had one day with Mr. G, the instructor of the course, he promised me that if I would get this HVAC license, then I would never have to worry about coming back to prison because of a lack of money because there would always be a job available in this field.

I had always respected the way Mr. G treated us inmates with so much respect as men and not inmates, so I took him up on his offer and joined his program. I also figured that keeping my mind occupied with taking classes would help my remaining years go by a lot faster than just sitting around and watching the paint dry on wet walls.

I completed the course with flying colors and received my HVAC Certification. I was even named to the Dean's List of Vance Granville Community College in 2006 with a 4.0 GPA. I was really excited about all of the opportunities that Mr. G had told the class that this certification could provide us.

While looking for my job at the halfway house, I went through the phone book and called every refrigeration company listed. I called and called, but I guess the fact that I was recently released from prison and still living in the halfway house with limited constrictions and mobility didn't seem to appealing to the companies that I had called.

I was beginning to get nervous because I knew that if I didn't find a job soon, I could possibly be sent back to prison to finish the remainder of my six months behind the walls again. I even gave up on the refrigeration idea, and just started calling companies I figured it would be easy for me to get a job at, but even still, I would often be denied because of the three felonies, violence and gun charges I had in my criminal records.

My case manager began to pressure me daily about not having a job as of yet. I began to get frustrated and had already accepted going back to prison, so I told her to send me back, it didn't matter to me, I had already done over four years, so what did I care about another six months. But the truth was, I did care and the last thing I wanted was to leave even the little bit of freedom I had again.

I began calling companies that I had already called two and three times before asking if there were any changes and if they needed any help, regardless of what they would pay me, I just wanted to stay free.

No after No, then the blessing came, one of the commercial refrigeration companies I had called days before invited me in for an interview for the next day. I was excited and afraid all at the same time. I wanted and needed the job, but in the thirty years of my life, I had never been on a job interview.

The next day, I jumped on the bus heading towards Watson Refrigeration for my interview. Not familiar with the bus system, I didn't know that the bus wouldn't drop me off where the business was actually located. The bus route stopped on New Bern Avenue at the Wal-Mart, and I was going to have to walk the rest of the way, which was about five miles down New Hope Rd. going towards Poole Rd.

Some guys I was with on the bus from the halfway house questioned if I was going to actually walk five miles down the road in a full suit in the blazing ninety-eight degree sun. I never replied, I just started walking and praying.

When I arrived to the company, I was tired and drenched in sweat. The receptionist offered me some water and paper towels to wipe my face. I was truly embarrassed to arrive to the interview in this manner, but at least I was there. Moments later, the owner of the company walked in the door and just looked at me in amazement. I think the fact I was coming to apply for a refrigeration job in a full suit threw him off a little, then to see me sitting there drenched in sweat as if I had been swimming.

He took me into his office and just began talking to me about his life and some of the guys that worked for him. I didn't say much; I guess I wasn't sure if this was the normal process of a job interview. He continued to tell me that he admired the fact that I was so determined to get a job, that I walked those five miles of blazing sun in a full suite. He said to me that everyone needs a second chance in life from time to time and that he was willing to give me mine.

Not only did Chuck bless me with a job that day, he also blessed me with the encouragement to never give up and inspired me to keep pushing forward. I'm not sure if he even understood the impact that he had on my current situation and life.

I was happy that I had finally found a job, but I was even happier that he offered to give me a ride back up to the Wal-Mart so I could catch the bus back to the hallway-house. I learned that where there is a will, there is away, and when there is no way, God will always make a way for you if you stay faithful.

I started working at Watson Refrigeration the following week earning $7.50 per hour. Initially, I served as Helper, meaning that I didn't do any of the installer work such as Reading Blueprints, Hanging Refrigeration Units, Running, Fitting or Welding

Refrigeration Pipe Lines. My only duty at that time was to hand the other guys whatever tools they needed and to go and get whatever copper pipe they needed.

I hated being a helper. I had never done any manual labor in my life; therefore I was truly ignorant to what any tools such as channel locks where, so when they yelled for me to throw them certain tools, the dumbfounded look on my face often gave the guys a good laugh.

I also hated having to be the one going to fetch the copper pipe needed from out of the container. They would yell down to me from the scissor lift the sizes they need to run their hang. "Sean, I need three 7/8's – six 1 1/8's", and so on, and I had to run out inside the hot blazing container that normally sat fifty to hundred yards away from the building we where working in and grab forty to fifty pounds of copper pipe on my shoulder and bring it to them.

It's ironic to look back now and realize that within all of the hate I had for being a Helper, it is where I found my love for learning.

PJ, my supervisor at the time, who was also younger than me said something to me one day on the ride back to the halfway house that would change my mindset and life forever. He mentioned the fact that he noticed how the other guys were giving me a hard time because I didn't know my copper pipe sizes or the names of the tools they worked with. He told me they would continue to do so until I did and not to take it to personal, because that's the way they break in all rookies to the team.

As I began to get out of the truck, PJ assured me that "The More You Know, The More You Will Grow". From that day forward I made it my mission to learn everything I could concerning the refrigeration industry. I realized that the only way for me not to be a Helper anymore was for me move myself above the skill level and demand of a Helper. It was apparent to me that the very obstacle I had to overcome was my ignorance of the industry.

Everyday, I started asking more questions at work. I wanted to learn everything. I stood side by side of PJ and asked him questions while he was reading the blueprints. I started watching the guys closely as they begin to weld. I studied them turning on the torches, how they held the torch and the silver in their process of welding. I even gained the courage to ask one of the guys to let me try it, and he did.

I began studying the blueprints daily, even though I had no idea what I was looking at. I practiced welding on old copper pipes and fittings until I became comfortable at going at it on my own.

Eight or nine months had gone by and I noticed that I was slowly but surely moving out of the Helpers position to becoming an Installer. After a year or so, I was running on my own. PJ would give me my task for the day and I would do my part to get the job done.

I had learned so much and was truly happy that I was no longer a Helper. At this point, I even had my own Helper, but unfortunately, I was still making the same $7.50 per hour, while finding out later through the grapevine that my Helper had been started off at $8.00 per hour.

The next morning before leaving out from the shop to the construction site, I went to talk to Chuck about my pay rate. I informed him of my growth of knowledge and skillset of my job, and he simply replied, "Yeah I Know, PJ told me how well you are doing".

Joy filled me with his recognition of my hard work that I had put in to climb the company ladder.

Without debate or further conversation, Chuck raised my pay rate to $9.00 per hour. He then said to me, "I've been wondering when you was going to come and ask for a raise. Nobody will offer you more in life, until you desire more for yourself".

During the next seven years I worked in the Commercial Refrigeration industry between the companies of Watson Refrigeration and Goodwin Refrigeration. I had gone from being a Helper knowing nothing to a Foreman traveling the country with my own crew of guys working on Commercial Refrigeration projects for Sam Clubs and Wal-Mart's. I went from starting off at $7.50 per hour to earning $20.00 per hour by the time I left the refrigeration industry for the last time, which was due to me being laid off due to the economy crisis and job losses.

I had more than paid my dues to deserve my growth within the refrigeration industry. Some days I would jump in the truck in North Carolina with my guys and drive twelve hours to a Wal-Mart in Florida, only to jump straight out of the truck and go to work for another ten to twelve hours. I've even seen days where me and my guys would work twenty-two hours straight and then would have to drive ten plus hours back home.

Though disappointed by the lay off, I found comfort in the realization that If I could start from the bottom and work so hard to work myself to the top for someone else and their company, then I could surly do it for myself and my own company. I learned to overcome my obstacles of ignorance, which truly allowed me to grow more based off the more I would know.

Thinking back reminds me of a fortune cookie I once read that said, "If you don't have a plan for your life, then somebody else will".

"You Can't Have a Testimony Without Being Tested"

Lesson 3

"Survive your Struggle"

SURVIVE

To remain alive or in existence;

1. To continue life or activity
2. To live, exist, or remain active beyond the extent of

STRUGGLE

2. To be strenuously engaged with a problem, task, undertaking, or the like.
3. To make a strenuous effort; strive
4. To contend against
5. To progress or penetrate with difficulty

(Defined by The American Heritage Dictionary of the English Language)

It is inevitable that we will go through struggles in life. I love mild temperature sunny days, as oppose to very hot or cold days, nonetheless, cold rainy days. I would also have to agree with the fact that in life, I have seen more cold rainy days than sunny. As I think about the fact, I also have to contemplate the truth that without rain, there would be no growth. Without water, there would be no life.

Too much of anything is harmful, especially water. Just as water allows life, it also brings death. Excessive water to a plant drowns the plant in the same way a person can drown from engulfing too much water into their lungs. The struggle is no different. If we allow our struggles to drown us, then we will surely die, be it by the cause of suicide, stress or illness. In order to thrive in life, we must learn how to survive our struggles.

I remember vividly the moment I came closest to committing suicide. I can still feel the heart ache and hear the conversation within my mind. I was beyond tired of being tired. I felt hopeless. I had reached the point that I wasn't even angry anymore, but yet numb and defeated. All that went through my mind was the questions of, what's the point of fighting anymore and who would even miss me and why?

Of course I thought about my grandmother and all others that was closest to me who without doubt I knew loved me. I went back and forth with myself, convincing myself that I would actually be helping them rather than hurting them by taking away me as an extra burden in their life.

I began to speed up my truck, with the intent of driving off the deep bank of Highway 264 between Raleigh and Wilson, NC. I saw the perfect area that was a deep drop and lined with a tree line at the bottom of the embankment. I had made up my mind that I was going to do it. I speed up to 95mph, and just as fast as I snatched my steering wheel to the right to run off the road, God snatched it back to the left and swerved me back on course.

Still no tears, only questions, subconsciously coming from a higher level of thought process than my own. I know within my soul that it was God questioning me; therefore I will say God asked,

"Are you a slave to the world and others or are you the master of yourself? If you are indeed the master of yourself, then who am I? Am I not the King of Kings, Lord of Lords and Master of Masters? Am I not he who created you, therefore what gives you or anyone else the right to destroy you?"

Those questions pierced my heart and soul. Questions and thoughts began to overwhelm my mind. I could clearly hear the thoughts in which God spoke to me.

"I have given you great gifts and talents, but yet you rather dismiss your purpose for having them and abort the mission in which I have personally chosen you for. I have allowed you to bear your burdens in order to make you strong. I have planted your feet in quicksand in order to get you familiar with the unstable grounds you will continue to walk on during your journey. Your struggles are to strengthen you and remind you that you will always need me."

I will be honest and admit that I truly didn't understand most of the thoughts I had coming in and going out of my mind so frantically. I wasn't yet at a level of understanding to comprehend the significance of Gods words. It wasn't until years later when I was in prison walking the track that I had such an epiphany and began to understand the salvation within my struggles.

It seems, all my life, all I have known is struggle. The struggle of being poor. The struggle of wanting to be loved by a mother and father who abandoned me to the struggle. The struggle of feeling like a failure when it seemed so often that I couldn't win from losing. The struggle of wanting to be more than the nothing I was, but how could I change my situation, if I couldn't change my situation.

My struggles begin to suffocate my happiness, kidnapping my smile and laughter. My love slowly turned into hate for myself. I hated the struggle; therefore I began to hate life. I hated me for being the cause of my struggle.

I once wrote a poem that said, "What I thought to be trials and tribulations was actually the misunderstanding of Gods lessons, and what I thought to be heart ache and pain was only the preparation for Gods blessings"

It took me many years of my life to begin to understand that all of the struggles that God had allowed me to survive in life was only to strengthen me. I learned from every struggle. I then began to learn to accept and appreciate every struggle. I learned to utilize my struggles as stepping-stones to my success.

Within every struggle, there is a key element of NEED in order for you to survive your struggle. That NEED is the NEED of God's grace and mercy in order for you to make it through. It's like suffocating, in order to survive, You NEED Air! Without struggle, sometimes we soon forget our NEED of God. When things are well in life, the thought of God's grace fades from our presence, but when turbulent trials arise, we always call on God for help.

Most forget that we serve a jealous God. Think of how it makes you feel when those certain people in your life "Only Call You When They Need You".

Imagine God saying, "I see how it is, you call me when you need me. You cry out my name when the struggle get real for you, but when it's all good your way, you forget about the ones who helped pull you through".

It's common for us to "Thank" someone after helping us through whatever situation, but how often do we "Thank" God, or anyone for that matter, for even standing side by side with us in the midst of the storm while the storm is raging at its highest peak.

Learn to "Thank" God for your struggles. Thank him for holding your hand while walking through and glorify him for allowing you to survive your struggle.

Step outside of your selfish being for a moment and think of all of the people who actually committed suicide because they didn't survive their struggle. They gave up on themselves and God.

I, just as you, have gone through many struggles in life, and the key words are "gone through". If we went through our struggles of the past, we can surly "get through" our struggles of the future.

Expect the unexpected and stay prepared to overcome every obstacle that will stand before you. Believe in the unbelievable and know that you are much more stronger and wiser than you have never imagined yourself to be because you have God on your side.

I think back on how my mindset would shift back and forth from fear, optimism, depression and courage during my years of incarceration. One moment I felt as if I could serve another thousand years if needed and refused to allow prison to break me mentally. The very next minute, I would feel as if I couldn't go on another second. I felt like breaking down and giving up. It was within those moments I learned to *Sanctify my Solitude.*

I will always proclaim that going to prison was indeed one of the best things that has ever happened to me in my life. It is within that struggle, I learned how mentally strong I was. It was then that I learned how intellectual I could be, if I allowed myself to be. It was then that I learned to love and appreciate myself.

Ironically, within my struggle of being physically bounded in prison is where I became mentally and spiritually "FREE". I found "Freedom" within "Bondage". Within the struggle of being taken away from myself, I Found Myself!

I wrote the very book, "The Passion of the Pen", that ultimately became my teaching tool and required reading text in my creative writing classes within the Wake County Public School System and my creative writing course at Sallie B. Howard school of the arts and education in Wilson, NC.

At the time of writing the book, it was my desire to break through the glass ceiling placed over my head of being just a street poet. I wanted to show and to prove to the world that I was indeed and intellectual also. It was my mission to break out of the box of just being a spoken word artist and prove that I could articulate my thoughts and ideas as a public speaker as well. I wanted to be acknowledged as a thinker. I wanted to be respected as a speaker and writer, who had more to talk about than just drugs, girls, hustling, and the struggle. I also had thoughts of spirituality, politics and solutions on how we can make our communities better.

As a child in grade school, it was my dream to write books to be taught in schools that little black kids like me could relate with and see themselves in the stories. I had always believed that the major cause of "illiteracy for black kids" was subject of not relating to the material we a forced to read in our schools. I wanted to write books that would tell our stories. I wanted to write books that we would be excited to read and learn from because within the story of the book, we would see our story also.

To God be the glory, within my struggle, I found success. I wrote my time away. Years faded as minutes when I took my mind off the struggle around and before me and focused only on my mission of writing the greatest work of literature I would have ever written. I challenged myself to be an intellectual. I challenged myself to write a book that would educate, inspire and invoke intrigue and emotions from my readers.

I pushed myself as writer harder than I ever had before. I studied the dictionary daily to increase my vocabulary. Nothing else even mattered to me other than becoming a better me.

I mentally left prison. I mentally escaped the grasp of my struggle of incarceration. I vowed to myself to become great.

Struggles are Situations and Circumstances. Situations and Circumstances are Temporary. I had to learn how to strategically get past the interim between struggle and success.

Stand strong in the face of your struggles. Welcome your struggles with open arms.

Appreciate the presence of your struggles. Accept the challenge of your struggle and fight with every ounce of fight you have within you to survive and succeed over your struggle.

"*I rather be*

Alone

Than to be without

God"

Lesson 4

"Sanctify your Solitude"

SANCTIFY
To reserve for sacred use:
1. To make holy; purify.
2. To make productive for holiness or blessing.

SOLITUDE
1. The state of being alone or remote from others.
2. A lonely or secluded place.

(Defined by The American Heritage Dictionary of the English Language)

While in prison waiting to be transferred from solitary confinement into general population, I stayed alone in my cell for twenty-eight days out of the thirty-five days I was there. During that alone time, I talked with God and myself, as well as listened. I prayed. I meditated. I reflected on my past. I envisioned my future. I stepped outside of myself and examined me as the rest of the world has always done.

Being the only child growing up with my grandmother, I became accustomed to being a loner. Most times, if I didn't have anyone to play with, I would be just fine playing with my vivid imaginations and creative thoughts. It didn't bother me at all being alone; it actually became my comfort zone and safe haven.

In time, I came to realize that my time alone in solitary confinement would become one of the best things that would have ever happened to me. It was there in that prison cell that I would once again hear the thoughts of God through an intimate conversation just as I had once before while driving down the highway contemplating suicide.

This time, my understanding of his words would allow me to comprehend everything that I didn't understand during our first conversation. The vision would become crystal clear.

As God spoke, I listened. As I questioned, God answered. Growing up, I was taught to never question God, but I never understood how anyone could ever get the answers they needed in life, without questioning.

I asked of God, "What do you want from me?"

God answered, "For you to spread my good news"

I questioned, "What good news and why me?"

God spoke, "That I am God and in the same way that I have and will continue to save you, I will save them"

I rebutted, "How have you saved me when all I have ever known in my life is struggle and pain. When all I ever wanted in life was to be able to truly smile. What good news do I have to tell anybody, when all I have ever lived and seen lived is a life of turmoil and hell."

God never negated the fact, but yet assured me that it was all part of his plan for me. His words to me spoke, "Only a Wolf can teach a Wolf how to live and survive as a Wolf".

It was then that I began to understand that I had to endure and go through hell myself in order for me to be able to help others find their way out of the depths of hell they are struggling to escape.

I will be the first to admit that I would have never chosen this mission for myself. I guess that's why in some ways, God never gave me a choice, but yet directed my every step towards this destined destination.

Within my creative writing workshops, I teach my students that in order for them to get through writers block, they must decrease their distractions.

Many of us suffer from an Attention Deficit Disorder, when it comes to staying focused on God. I myself get caught up in the struggle and my fight to hustle my way out. Instead of focusing on Gods love and guidance, I focus on the next phone call I need to make, the next meeting I need to attend, as well as all the responsibilities I have on the daily as a husband and father.

I have to stop and stand still sometimes just to slow my thoughts down from running rapid. I have to stop and refocus my sight on the vision that God has given me to manifest within my journey in life.

Allow your solitude to be your sanctuary. The very place where you find peace of mind. The quiet place where you can attentively listen and understand God's directions. Allow it to be your meeting place with yourself.

Find time to be alone. The amount of time is totally depending on your needs, even five minutes alone with yourself and God can rejuvenate your energy level to carry you throughout the rest of the day or week.

In the same way we have to make time for work, family, classes, phone conversations, facebook, movies, shopping and even eating, is the same way we have to dedicate time for ourselves and God.

As children, we fear even the thought of being alone. As adults, we still feel the same, but at some point in life when you realize that God is always with you through every situation, you should become comforted and fear shall fade away.

I now use every opportunity of solitude I can get to get closer to God and myself. As I drive my truck with no radio on, it allows me to think. When I cut grass or do yard work, I utilize that time also to think and concentrate on hearing the voice of God.

I indeed without question love the presence of my wife and daughters, but I also understand the need of being alone and without distractions.

Decrease your Distractions in order to block out outside interferences of confusion and chaos. Most often, others bring more confusion to your serene thoughts than you do to yourself. It's nothing disrespectful to anyone else about respecting yourself enough to enjoy being at peace with yourself.

Within silent thoughts is where I learned to recognize blessings. Blessings come in many forms, written, oral and visual, but if you don't have the focus to recognize the blessing when it appears or presents it's self to you, then it will surely pass you bye without the promise of ever returning again.

Daily I pray for the discernment to recognize the many blessings provided by God. Within the conversation with the homeless, within the smile of a child, within the lyrics of a song, within the moral of a movie, I hear God's voice and find my blessings.

You may ask, where do you find time in such a hectic daily schedule? Ironically, time is not found, but yet created. I create my **Me Time.** For Example, during a regular work and school day, my wife and daughters wake up around 6:30am. My oldest daughter gets on the bus at 7:30am, my wife leaves for work at 8am and my baby girl gets on the bus at 8:30am which allows me just enough time to leave my house and have the doors of The Sean Ingram Academy open by 9am.

Did I mention that between 6:30am and 8:00am is the time where I do my morning house chores such as take out the trash and wash the dishes, yes fellas, I wash the dishes in my house and even as a grown man you will still have house chores, even more of them than you did as a youth.

During this time I also design my business flyers, update my websites and App and create my email campaigns as well as check, respond and send out any emails that are pending.

With all of that being said and done, I create my Me Time of Solitude before my family even awakes. I awake between 4am and 5am. This is the time I Pray, Think, Reflect and Plan out my day.

I did it daily until it became just another part of my routine. Now I awake without thought, but yet by habit. Just as I once created bad habits, I now focus creating good habits for myself.

"No One Will Ever

Hold You Back

More Than

You Will Yourself"

Lesson 5

"Change your Challenge"

CHANGE – To cause to be different; alter. To give a completely different form or appearance; transform.

CHALLENGE – A call to engage in a contest or fight.

The quality of requiring full use of one's abilities, energy, or resources. A difficult task or problem: something that is hard to do.

(Defined by The American Heritage Dictionary of the English Language)

My grandmother always use to say to me that if you are going through hell, the last thing you want to do is stop and stay there, therefore against all odds you must keep going.

To live is to fight and to survive is to live to fight another day. I always say that if we are allowed another day, then we are allowed to have another chance. Another chance in life to **Optimize our Opportunities.** If we do not take advantage of our opportunity to seize the day, then we lessen our chances to succeed.

Challenges will come and go in life, at least they should, but I have found that some people who feel more comfortable in using excuses to validate their failures will refuse to change their challenge for the fear of no longer having that excusable kickstand to hold up their validity.

Your challenges could be a number of things, all piled up as burdens weighing on your shoulders bringing you down to your knees. We try our best to appear strong to rest of the world, but the truth is, second by second, we become weaker and weaker until we just can't carry the weight of our problems anymore, that's when we most often give out, give up and breakdown before breaking through.

Challenges would come, but would never go. I would just keep allowing my challenges to pile up, challenge by challenge. I had no resources to help my financial challenges, therefore the amounts owed to change my financial challenges kept adding up until I seemed to bury myself alive in debt.

Birthed from my financial challenges, all other sorts of challenges were born, such as emotional and low self-esteem issues. Financially struggling with low self-esteem and a lack of confidence that my situation could change for the better, I found myself digging myself deeper and deeper into a whole until I hit rock bottom.

I felt that it was truly me against the world. All my challenges now stood before me blocking me from seeing the light of day. My thoughts, judgments and rationale became eclipsed by confusion.

Being that all of my challenges before me at the time seemed to be financial, I figured the best way to solve them all at once was to make a lick (robbery) big enough to cover all of my debts at once.

Having no understanding of financial management, having no mentorship by any financial advisors, I did all that I knew to do.

At this point in my life, I was tired of fighting my financial challenges. I felt like I had one last fight in me and I was willing to die to give it all I got, for me, it was all or nothing.

In the midst of all the chaos and confusion going on in my life at the time, I accepted the invitation to being a part of a bank robbery. I had made up my mind that if it was going to be, now was the time, win or lose, because I was more than tired of fighting and failing.

Due to the respect and confidentiality of my co-defendants, I will not go into detail concerning the bank robbery, but needless to say, it wasn't a success. Instead of eliminating all the challenges I had before me, I only added more and more to the enormous pile that already existed.

I found myself in a federal prison paying back ten thousand dollar restitution from the wages of eight cents an hour, which totaled six dollars a month.

It seemed as if the black hole I had feel in had closed. I couldn't see the light of day. When I looked in the mirror, I saw the face of failure in the reflection.

What was I to do? What could I do?

I have always asked the question, how can you change your situation if you can't change your situation? Exactly! In order to change your situation, you must *change* your situation. Therefore you have to **Stop Stressing and Start Strategizing**.

In my opinion, stress is the greatest catalyst of failure. Think about it, when a person starts to stress, it often slows or even stops their drive, their ambition, their progression and even their desire and confidence that they can actually succeed despite the obstacles that stand before them.

The simple solution to this problem is to never give up and go for broke until you slowly but surely begin changing your situation.

Persevere your Process and stay focused on achieving your goal. Understand that your process and timeline may be very different from others, so only give attention to your situation and not jump into a race of competition with anyone else. Meaning, mind your own business. Never forget, that your life is your business. Only Compete with yourself and your own Capabilities.

The struggle is real, make no doubt about it, but the struggle is a situation and the situation can be changed. It may take months or even years, but in time and over time it will change.

What I'm going to say next is definitely easier said than done, but it's a must. You have to go for broke, meaning that you have to sacrifice it all. You have to be willing to go hungry. In business while building that business, most owners pay employees bi-weekly without ever paying themselves for the first two to five years.

Every cent you make, reinvest it back into your business. Allow every dime you make help you pay off old debts that will in time bring you out of your financial whole. Trust me as crazy as it may sound, a dime a day will eventually eat away a ten thousand dollar balance. Yes, it will take years, but it will happen.

Going for broke will also mean that you will be broke. Sacrifices must be made. No vacations. No clothing shopping sprees. No cable TV. No eating out for lunch everyday with your co-workers. Whatever sacrifices you must make in order to change your challenge, do what's needed in order to achieve your long-term goals.

I go for broke, because I AM BROKE. Even as I write this book, I am broke, but I can also say that I'm far from being poor. Please understand that there is a major difference in being BROKE and being POOR.

My personal definitions are, Broke is having no money or finances. Poor is having no options or opportunities. Being broke is a situation. Being poor is a circumstance. Being broke is a choice. Being poor is a state of mind.

I grew up poor and while in that poor mindset, I thought college wasn't for me because I was poor. I never recognized that I could afford college because I was broke and all I needed to do was find the financial means and resources to go to college. I didn't believe in my poor state of mind that pell grants, student loans or the many other financial assistance opportunities were for poor people.

Now as a broke businessman, my goal and job everyday is to find finances to continue to build my business until my business builds me.

Stay focused and disciplined to change your situation penny after penny, dime after dime. Go for broke and be proud of being broke because you see the bigger picture and understand the method to your madness.

Unfortunately, very few, if any will understand or believe in you. You will be considered crazy. Prayers will seem as if they are going unanswered. Your trust and faith in yourself and others will begin to dissipate.

Trust Me, stay FOCUSED and Follow One Course Until Successful.

Continue to look and GO forward even if you have to GO alone.

"Birthed From My Chaos

Was Born

Gods Gift of Clarity"

Lesson 6

"Simplify your System"

SIMPLIFY

To make simple or simpler;
1. Render less intricate or complex.

SYSTEM

A group of interacting, interrelated, or interdependent elements forming or regarded as forming a collective entity.

(Defined by The American Heritage Dictionary of the English Language)

Complexity is defined as a combination of components equating to something that is difficult.

In mathematics, even the most complex mathematical problem has a solution. Our job is to find the solution of the problem. Within the process of finding the solution, we may have to solve a number of small problems within the system of solving the major problem.

This is my process of **Simplifying your System.** The first step to simplifying your system is **Decreasing your Distractions.**

In order to stay focused on your mission and block out confusion and chaos from cluttering and distracting your thought process, you must be willing to sacrifice a number of liable relationships (relationships that are liabilities and not assets) with people you may now have or have had in the past.

Whether it's your mother, father, wife, husband, sister, brother, or all the way down the line to your closest childhood friend, if that person doesn't support you, has your best interest in mind, or bring value of advice and experience when it comes to you and your mission, leave their opinions as opinions.

It's a hard pill to sometimes swallow, but the fact of the matter is that everybody that hugs you and smiles in your face does not have your best interest at heart or truly wants to see you succeed. Accept this fact and you will be much better off in life.

In no way to sound skeptical of mixing personal and business relationships, but just because your mother loves you dearly as her child doesn't mean that her motherly love will make her a good business manager or partner for you.

More often than not, you will stand in a very small group of people who will even remotely understand the journey you are on in life, and those are the people you are in need of connecting with. Your father must always be your father, but he doesn't have to be your business mentor.

Distractions can be a number of things, but I believe that the number one distraction you have to decrease from your thought process is negativity.

Negativity will destroy your focus, drive and dreams. Therefore, to the best of your ability, keep all negative people, conversations, situations and circumstances to a minimum and away from you.

If you have that family member, friend or co-worker who is always in a bad mood or always has something negative to say when asked how are they are doing, respectfully leave them standing where they stand and begin to walk away from them in a different direction as soon as possible.

In your journey to success, everyone you encounter will be more than happy and willing to tell you what you should be, or need to be doing. Remember, it's always easier said than done to the person who has never done it or doesn't have to do it. Remember, there is a major difference in the mindset and understanding of an employee as opposed to someone who is self-employed or a business owner.

My next step to this process is only focusing on one challenge at a time. Regardless of how many obstacles or hurdles you have in front of you, you can only jump one at a time. Always be disciplined to Stay Focused and Follow One Course Until Successful.

Looking at the BIG PICTURE is sometimes dangerous. Sometimes the big picture looks very complex and complicated to solve. Most times when we look at the complexity of the big picture, it overwhelms us and we begin to doubt our ability to solve the big problem instead of focusing on solving the small problems we know we can with ease.

In 1997, one of my many God-Mothers, Theresa Edwards, informed me with the upmost love and sincerity that the biggest problem I had at the time was the fact that I was too talented and poorly disciplined when it comes to completing task.

I agreed and had no rebuttal to reply. She hit the nail directly on the head. I would begin a project, get bored, frustrated, or even see a new project that interested me more and never complete the previous project I had been working on.

Birthed from this revelation came my first book. She pleaded with me to just pick one mission or task and follow it through until the very end. I chose writing and publishing the book I had always dreamed of.

The only promises I made concerning completing this project was to God and myself.

I began writing and writing, day and night. Thoughts of "How am I going to publish this book?' came into my mind. Thoughts of "What money do I have to publish or promote this book?" came into my mind. Every negative thought I could imagine came into my mind until I finally erased them all and declared that "I will cross that bridge when I get to them, but for now, my only focus is to write".

After I had completed the book manuscript, it was time to look into the world of publishing.

There use to be a Books-A-Million bookstore on Wake Forest Road years ago. I would go to that bookstore seemingly every other day asking the manager questions and advice of what I needed to do to get my book on their bookshelf.

Every time she said she didn't know, I would politely say "Ok, Thank You" and return two or three days later with different questions that could still answer my primary question of "What do I need to do to get my book on a major bookstore shelf?"

Thank God she was such a sweet and courteous older lady, because I can only imagine the thoughts that ran through her mind when she saw me coming through the bookstore door.

Ironically enough, the manger at the bookstore never really did answer my questions, but this is when God stepped in and began to open closed doors.

While at the book store one day hunting for any book that could help me learn more about book publishing or finding a agent, a lady, complete stranger, who was not an employee of the bookstore asked me what I was looking for. She told me that she had noticed me from coming in a few times before. Her inviting spirit compelled me to open the floodgates to my frustrations of trying to figure out how to get this book published.

Note, learn to recognize when God comes into the mix. The lady listened intensely and smiled. She then asked, "Have you ever heard of self-publishing?"

"No mamm", I replied. She then began to pull out her cell phone while telling me the story of a cousin of hers son who had just self-published a book a few months ago and is now doing book signings at stores.

I can't even begin to tell you how excited I was. It seemed as if it was to good to be true, but it indeed was. After her conversation, she wrote down the name Lightning Source on a piece of paper and told me to go home and research them because this is the place her cousin's son had self-published with.

Overwhelmed with adrenaline, it seemed as if I couldn't get home fast enough. I rushed directly to my computer and looked up this company Lightning Source. As I read though the website, my heart began betting faster and faster, for low and behold, the beginning of my self-publishing journey had begun.

I had finally crossed that long bridge high in the sky above raging waters with planks falling with every step I took. Now my focus turns to the next bridge to come.

"Never Allow

Your Ignorance

To Eclipse

Your Intellect"

Lesson 7

"Master your Mindset"

MASTER

The man who has control over another or others.
1. A man of great learning, scholar:

MINDSET

The established set of attitudes held by someone.
1. The fixed state of how a person thinks and perceives, thought process.

(Defined by The American Heritage Dictionary of the English Language)

I heard Oprah Winfrey once say that she had always wanted to OWN herself. In my mind that is the true definition of freedom and independence. Her words changed my mindset. My mission became to become the master of myself and master my own mindset. I no longer wanted to be a slave to anyone else, not financially, emotionally, physically and especially not mentally.

When we think of the word Master, many of us African Americans commonly think of the title Master before acknowledging the definition of the word Master. We generally think of ownership instead of being greatly skilled. I myself, even now think first of the title Master, before the word Master, which both coincide with the underscored definition of the words ambivalent meaning.

One of the greatest articles of historical writings I have ever read other than the bible is "Making of a Slave" by William Lynch. In this letter to American Slave Masters, Willie Lynch instructs in detail the step by step process of mentally destroying the African American male and rebuilding him to be a loyal, faithful and obedient slave until the end of his days.

Willie Lynch also understood that with the Male being head of household and leader of his community, that if you broke him properly, then everyone else that would follow him would also be subconsciously broken. When the wife of the man see her husband being broken, she becomes broken, then in synch, their children become broken and now you have an entire household of slaves. Multiply this process house by house through out an entire community, neighborhood, county and state and now you have a stronghold on slavery.

Understanding the methodology of the Willie Lynch letter, I now understand that the only way to reverse the slave mentality is to break down the slave mentally/mindset and rebuild him back to being the Intellectual he was born to be.

It is said that we will be what we see, and if indeed I grew up looking at those who I love, admire and depended on for protection being subjected to being a slave, I would fall in line to what I know and see. In the same, if I grew up seeing my mother and father owning their own business, or obtaining high-ranking management positions in fortune five hundred corporations, my perspective of expectations would be a lot different.

As I look back on my life, I think of all of the negative thoughts, emotions and perspectives that kept me enslaved. Low self-esteem lowered my expectations of myself, therefore I restrained my growth more than anyone else ever could.

Within the process of changing my mindset, I began to understand that I also had to change everything else around me. Not only did I have to change the visuals, conversations and literature that I partook, but also the environments I navigated on a frequent basis.

I had to change the groups of people that I associated myself with on a daily basis. I found myself examining every friend or relationship I had with a person in order to prioritize his or her purpose and position in my life.

Many may consider me as a socialist, and in some ways, they may be correct, but studies prove that on average, most groups of people who associate with each other on a daily basis earn no more than five thousand dollars, up or down, apart from each other.

Therefore, when it comes to intellectual conversations concerning whatever field, market place or career path you choose in life, in order to maximize the potential of your educational conversations, you have to converse with those with like minds on an equal or greater level of understanding than you.

Learn to master your mindset and you will find the key to unlock the doors to your potential.

Through study, I have learned that in order to become a master of a skill, you must first put in ten thousand hours of hard work, practice and dedication to bettering your skillset.

Imagine, ten thousand hours of constantly playing the piano, studying law books, shooting free throws or writing word after word after word.

My mission is to become a master at what I do. My mission is to be the best me that I can be. My mission is to own myself. My mission is to master my mindset.

Unfortunately, even though I was only in prison a few years compared to many others, I am indeed institutionalized. At times, I still think like a criminal. Being a hustler is instilled into the very core of my being and it's like detoxing cold turkey to get these thoughts and feelings out of me.

Trust me when I tell you that everyday I work hard just to stay focused and keep on track. Please believe me when I say that despite all that I've accomplished since leaving prison, I know that I am only one wrong step and decision away from going back.

During my conviction at sentencing, Judge Terrance Boyle, assured me that if I came back before him in life, or any other judge for that matter, I would receive twenty five years to start, then he would add on the time for whatever charges I would be served with.

I know and understand my position in life. I know what holes in the road wait ahead of me and what will happen if I make that wrong step.

Regardless of what other people do or say, I have to be accountable for my own thoughts and actions. Nobody other than me can convince or make me do anything.

Master your mindset. See the positive within the negative. Find the solution within the problem. Never allow your ignorance to eclipse your intellect.

I truly believe that in order to be it, you must first believe it; therefore I strongly encourage you to believe in the unbelievable. Believe in You.

No one could ever truly believe in you, until they can truly believe that you believe in you first. Your belief in yourself will compel others to believe in you also.

It's simply *The Law of Attraction*. Naturally people are attracted to strength, confidence, power, and the lights that shine the brightest.

Let all those things and more be in the make up of the characteristics and traits you posses.

Believe It and You Will Be It...

"One Day

a Great Opportunity

Will Come Knocking

At Your Door,

But Will You Be Ready

When That Day Comes"

Lesson 8

"Specialize your Skillset"

SPECIALIZE

Concentrate on and become expert in a particular subject or skill:

1. Confine oneself to providing a particular product or service:

2. Make a habit of engaging in a particular activity.

SKILLSET

A particular combination of skills that a person has developed over time.

1. A person's range of skills or abilities:

(Defined by The American Heritage Dictionary of the English Language)

Privileged with an opportunity to stand side by side with Dr. Calvin Mackie while speaking at a helping hands youth summer camp seminar for the Wake County Public School System, I went from being a mentor to being a mentee all in the same breathe.

Dr. Mackie spoke about the importance of understanding Mindset, Skillset, and becoming an Asset. The way he explained it provided me with a new vision of comprehension of why the thin line between the successful and unsuccessful seems so thick. Many possess great skills, but only a few specialize their skillset in order to separate and elevate themselves from others who may have similar skills.

Just as there are a million and more spoken word artist, there are a billion and more motivational speakers, but there is only one Sean Ingram. I do look at others in my field of expertise with admiration of their movements and success, but I only compete with myself, pushing me to be a better me tomorrow than I am today.

Without question, I'm by no means the most articulate, the most educated and surely not the most publicized or requested speaker, but undoubtedly, I am and will forever be the most passionate speaker that will ever be able to tell the testimonial story of Sean Ingram as I do. Many times people are amazed that during my speaking engagements I never read from a written speech or use notes, but why should I when everything I say is just a memory from the truth of my personal journey.

With each word I speak, I re-live every emotion I felt in the past of that particular moment and passionately orate it in the present in order for my audience to visually see and emotionally feel now what I felt then.

Understand your uniqueness and specialize your skillset. Understand that every situation you have ever experienced, good or bad, positive or negative, beneficial or not has served as learning tools for you to add into your intellectual tool bag that will equip you with the necessary tools in order for you to enhance your skillset.

I once wrote a poem that says, "What I thought was trials and tribulations was actually the misunderstanding of Gods lessons, and what I thought of to be heart ache and pain was actually the preparation for Gods blessings" meaning that every instance that God allowed me to survive my struggle, it prepared me and made me mentally and emotionally stronger so that I can stand grounded as whom he has destined me to become.

Growing up in poverty, learning to live and deal with the emotions of anger, abandonment, loneliness, depression and confusion, living to die by running towards death in the streets as fast as I could, which ultimately led me to serving time in prison prepared me to be the author, educator, actor, spoken word artist and motivational speaker that I am now.

Never minimize the major moments that had happened in your life, learn from it in order to grow from it and allow it to justify your journey.

When I first started performing as a spoken word artist, I stood on the stage crying out my soul through words. I released all of my pain, all of my frustration and all of my confusion through my poems. At first, it confused me when the audience applauded in standing ovation as if being happy about my turmoil in life.

I would often confide in my poetic brothers Langston Fuze and Dasan Ahanu. I still remember our many conversations as we traveled up and down the roads, to and from every open mic we could find. I can still hear Dasan explain to me the reasons why the crowds never uttered a word during my performances, or often wouldn't even clap when I finished each poem, but why the eruptions of ovations came at the end of my performance. He explained that because of my word play and the way I wrote in riddles, I mentally leave the audience a verse or two behind. He said that when I would get to verse four or five, the audience would still be stuck on verse two or three and find themselves lost and trying to play catch up.

Fuze would explain how the crowed would be amazed with my delivery and conviction. He proclaimed that my greatest gift to performing was not being a performer at all, but simply a guy speaking with passion from the depths of his soul. Fuze even nicknamed me "Down Home" because of my personable approach to performing. He said that I always allowed the audience to relate to a real life person rather than being entertained by just a performer.

Fuze and Dasan taught me to be me. They taught me to speak my truth and always encouraged me to stay true to my truth, regardless how anyone else felt about it.

I found as I continued to grow as a spoken word artist that my truth was my specialty.

My specialty became the ability to invoke emotions. My ability to Inspire, Motivate, Educate and make you Cry all in the same breathe became my forte. I truly became the author, and made the audience, or person reading my work, feel anyway that I desired them to feel. I put them on that emotional rollercoaster in which they would ride until, I as the conductor, ended their ride.

When I was first introduced with the opportunity to work with the Wake County Public School System and provide mentoring programs for many of our at-risk-youth. I was often questioned by the powers that be, of what skills did I have to work this particular group of kids?

Initially, their questions stumbled me because I had no degrees in this field or any special training for that matter, but after weeks and weeks of thought, the answer hit me like a train. My skills and specialty was that I could speak the same language as these kids. I could relate to their emotions and situations, which in turn made them relate to and respect me.

I have always proclaimed that you cannot teach a child, until you can reach that child. My gift was that I Could Reach That Child. We could relate to each other mentally and emotionally. Because we found grounds that we could relate to each other on, we found the perfect foundation to begin building our relationship on.

When questioned again, "Why me?" my response became, "Why Not Me?" and who better than me that have traveled the road they are now on and can successfully guide them from all of the pitfalls that lay before them while walking in their dark world. Who better to inspire them than someone they can relate to and say to themselves, that if he made it, then I can also? I am their example of the possibility.

True, I didn't go to a four year university for my higher learning of education, but I am assured that the fours years I spent in a federal prison educating my myself of myself was just as valuable.

"My Positive Energy

Has No Power Outlet

For Your Negative Attitude"

Lesson 9

"Decrease your Distractions"

DECREASE

Make or become smaller or fewer in size, amount, intensity, or degree:

DISTRACTIONS

1. A thing that prevents someone from giving full attention to something else.
2. Extreme agitation of the mind or emotions.

(Defined by The American Heritage Dictionary of the English Language)

Being destined is not the luck of the draw or something that happens just by chance. Your destiny is your preordained future manifested through your purpose in life. We all are destined for greatness, but unfortunately, everyone will never complete their journey in order to fulfill their prophecy.

Many of us pack our bags as adolescents with all of the tools and survival essentials needed to begin our journey towards greatness; but more often than many, we become side tracked by others and get derailed from staying on our path. We continue to live going down this detoured road, which leads us further and further away from the direction of our destiny.

When I was in prison, a good friend of mine who was a five-percenter broke down the knowledge of what the word focus meant. Being the wordsmith that I was, I was more than curious to find out what he was going to inform me of that would blow my mind as he so passionately proclaimed, I was truly unaware that this revelation would change my mindset and life forever. He told me that the acronym for FOCUS was Follow One Course Until Successful.

From that moment forward, I pledged to God and myself to never lose sight or focus from being the great writer, educator and motivational speaker that I knew in my soul I was destined to be. I vowed not to become distracted and get detoured off the road to my success.

Despite the obstacles that stood in my way, and the many detours that were readily available. Despite the potholes and unpaved trenches. Despite the many trees, branches and debris laying across the road from the storms in my life.

Despite the many hitchhikers that stood on the sidelines waving their arms to get my attention with their thumbs up, whose sole intention was to take me off of course. I kept going in the direction I knew I needed and never once turned around regardless of how fearful, uncomfortable or compassable confusing my journey became.

Learn the practice of having tunnel vision early on your race, you will need that experience later, because the closer you get to your finish line, the more distractions you will face that will desire to slow you down, with its goal of eventually stopping you.

I know that I'm on my right path for success because the Devil has never attacked me before, as he has now. Satan has never been more vigilant in the disruption of Gods plan for me.

Thinking back even over the process of writing this book you are now reading, I have had to overcome more obstacles and decrease more distractions than I ever had with my previous four books altogether.

Often I felt like Job in the bible. Knowing that this book would help save lives, the Devils desire was to stop me from publishing it by any means necessary.

He hit me with everything he could. Financial Problems, Family Issues, Health Issues, Business Stress, and even Marital Stress that drove in a wedge almost to the point of separation.

I felt overwhelmed. I felt like giving up. I felt that it wasn't worth it anymore. I then remembered the story of Job.

I realized that God had allowed Satan to do all these things to Job in order to test his faith, but the one demand that God had, was that Satan could not take Jobs life.

In order to have a TESTimony, you first must endure the TEST. I then began to realize and understand why it was so important to Satan that he stop this project. Satan came to kill, steal, and destroy. He is just doing what he does best, therefore I must also do what I do best, and that is to fight and overcome against all odds.

I became distracted by all of Satan's attempts to stop me from writing. I stop focusing on Gods purpose of me writing my autobiography and allowed my focus turn back towards all the problems I had knocking on my door.

Time after time, I stopped writing to get up to answer the door. Each argument at the door took my mind further away my thought process I had when I was writing.

The problem would temporarily leave until another problem came to stand in his very footsteps. Again, I would stop writing and go face the problem head on with every ounce of fight I had in me.

I would often go back to my writer's chair exhausted. Mentally and physically tired, most often to tired to continue writing or mentally find the thought I had left to answer the door to confront my consistent problems.

When there are no problems knocking on my door, bill collectors are constantly calling my phone. I answer only to answer the same argument, time after time, day after day.

Our Brains are the same as computers. I have Mac computers because of the Music and Design work I do on a daily basis. Mac computers are ideal for being a lot faster and handling a lot more storage than your personal computers for home or office use.

Ideally, our Mac is the best because it the strongest, but even a Mac will crash if overloaded. If I was to never clean my hard drive, then slowly but surely my Mac Boo Pro will begin to slow down until ultimately crashes and stops working, forever.

In essence, we are the same. Our human brains can only take but so much before giving out, which is described by passing out or fainting.

Negative Distractions often overload us, and until when can learn to decrease our distractions and clean some of that negative trash from our brains, we will never be able to function at 100% and reach our fullest potential.

"To Be a Great Leader

Is To Be

A Greater Servant"

Lesson 10

"Recognize your Reason"

RECOGNIZE
1. To perceive or acknowledge the validity or reality of:
2. To acknowledge, approve of, or appreciate:

REASON
1. The basis or motive for an action, decision, or conviction.

(Defined by The American Heritage Dictionary of the English Language)

What ever you choose to do in life, continue to do it for the reason you first began to do it. Do it because of the love you first had with it, and the same passion you started out doing it with.

Remember your reason day in and day out. Stay true to your truth because it will keep you from giving up when times will seem if they are too much for you to bear.

I can't honestly remember the day I found out I had a gift with putting together words, but I do remember always being a big dreamer and having these crazy ideas, even since my childhood.

I first started writing because I just had so much anger in me that I wanted to get it off my chest. I wanted to argue with my mom and dad and say curse words that I knew my grandma wouldn't allow, so I wrote my on paper just to get it out, then I would throw the papers away to keep from getting caught and getting in trouble.

The dream of being a writer was never mine, but that of my close childhood friend, David Sherrod, and my little cousin JJ Thompson.

I truthfully learned how to rhyme from them. I now feel like I have to make this dream of theirs become a reality through me because both of them died before reaching the ages of 25.

David and his cousin Dion would come over my house everyday to tell me their raps. I was more like the Puff Daddy of the group. The one who was gonna market and promote them until they hit big. My bedroom was smaller than small, but often would hold every kid in the neighborhood that was willing to rap.

I can still hear my grandfather yelling from the living room to "Keep All That Fuss Down, I can't Even Hear The TV That's Right In Front Of Me!"

The first time I was introduced to a real possibility of me being a writer was when I was in high school. I was writing a poem called "Daddy Stop The Cycle" just expressing all my anguish towards my daddy for never being a father, but the promise to myself that my children will never go through what I did as child because I would be there for them, regardless of any situation.

I got caught writing this poem while I suppose to be studying for a social studies test. My teacher took my note pad.

Later that day, I was called to the office concerning the poem I had written. They seemed to care more about if I had indeed written the poem rather than being in trouble for not studying, I truthfully was confused. I was no stranger to the principles office at all, but this time felt much different for me.

I really got confused when I saw Ms. Sutton walk into the office. She was never my teacher, but always a close friend to the family and a mother figure at school to all of us at-risk-kids.

She made me write her a poem every week. She believed in me as a writer before I even understood the gift I had. She then teamed up with my English teacher, Mr. Clark, who cultivated my thought process and taught me think outside the box.

Being the hustla that I was, I started hustling my gift by writing greeting cards for friends and other students in the school. I had a friend that could draw really good, so I had him draw flowers, hearts or anything that complemented the occasion on one side of the paper, and I would write what they wanted to say but didn't know how as a poem on the inside.

I then had the idea of writing books because I truly felt young black kids didn't like to read because we could never relate or see ourselves in what they made us read in school. I thought that if we liked reading, then we would be more willing to do our class and home work, which would allow us the chance to have better grades.

After I made a few personalized greeting card sales, I saw the vision of how I could bring my grandma and me out of the poverty we was bound in. I was planning to write us to freedom from the slavery we had always known.

When my grandma passed in 2014, I almost lost my reason. I almost lost my passion and drive to succeed as a writer. The journey has been rugged. I almost forgot my why, and gave up on the dream.

When David died, I felt like putting the pen down because it was truly his dream and not mine. When JJ died, I lost inspiration, because rapping never made me smile like it did him.

I thought about the days when I was house arrest and we would spend the entire day rhyming. My small room would be packed. My thoughts of going to prison shortly even faded away.

JJ, Roscoe, Matthew, Justin and me would rap all day with the memory of David in our hearts and mind.

I then remembered not long ago. I'm still doing it for them. I do it for my grandma who always believed in me no matter what. I do it for Ms. Alberta Sutton and Mr. Donald Clark because they believed in my writing ability even before I did, and they fought with me to better my gift. I do this for David and JJ, and have promised to never let their dream die.

"Visions Are Mirages,

That Only You

Can Sometimes See"

Lesson 11

"Visualize your Victory"

VISUALIZE

Form a mental image of; imagine.
1. Make something visible to the eye.

VICTORY

An act of defeating an enemy or opponent in a battle, game, or other competition.

(Defined by The American Heritage Dictionary of the English Language)

I know you have heard me say it more times than many that in order for you to be it, you first must believe it. I can never stress this fact enough.

I can't imagine Muhammed Ali visualizing himself losing in a boxing match. I can't imagine Michael Jordan visualizing himself missing the last second shot to win the game. I can't imagine Kobe Bryant visualizing himself being Sean Ingram on the basketball court in the NBA finals or championship game. I also can't imagine LeBron James not visualizing himself as being one of the greatest players to play basketball.

In order to Be It, You MUST See It. That visual has been burned into your brain. With every test, you must see that visual. Standing before every obstacle, you must see that visual of success behind it. With each heartbreak, you must see that visual of happiness in the near future to help mend your broken heart. Never take your eyes off your prize.

I think back to the "I have a dream" speech by Dr. Martin Luther King, Jr., when he proclaimed to the world that his eyes has seen the promise land, and even though he knew he would not step foot in that destined land in which he had journeyed so long to reach, he was well with death because he has seen the future. God had allowed him to see the visual of success from all of his hard work and effort to bring about change and equality for the African American people.

I think, without knowing, what's the reason to keep going? If I had listened to the many others who didn't believe in me or my dreams, I would have given up many years ago.

I've learned, that just as David in the bible, God sometimes only gives you a vision for only you to see and understand. If Noah was my father and he tried to explain the vision he saw to me, I would have thought he was crazy also.

What's Yours is Yours, also true with your Visions and Dreams. God will send the right people in your life that he has also shared the vision with to help and assist you.

Never lose sight of the victory line. Success is not about what you can do, but yet, about what you can endure. Keep your movement moving, no matter how tired you may become.

Champions have champion mindsets. They truly believe they will win. If not this year or next, I will win one of these times. When a champion loses, they don't give up and quit, they work harder, practice harder, and stay focused to be even be more prepared for their next opportunity to win the championship.

I know the vision that God gave me. I truly believe from the depths of my soul that it's no mirage. I know now that I'm only a step away from crossing my finish line.

Even with chaos and confusion still surrounding me, I rejoice and thank God allowing me the strength to persevere my process, which allowed me to not breakdown before I could reach my breakthrough.

Forty Years I have be on the training grounds for this very moment. Twenty years as an author, I have been on a mission to become an international best seller. I have ran the rugged race with grace and mercy on my side, even holding me up at times when my legs gave out from fatigue.

Evert second that I have spent specializing my skillset has prepared me for this very book.

In a world filled with Darkness, I never lost sight of that faded glimpse of light that attracted me in the beginning. In faith, I just closed my eyes and continued to walk towards it.

"Before You

Can Be It...

You Must First

Believe It"

Lesson 12

"Become your Belief"

BECOME
Begin to be.

BELIEF
1. An acceptance that a statement is true or that something exists.
2. Trust, faith, or confidence in someone or something.

(Defined by The American Heritage Dictionary of the English Language)

Trust me when I tell you that, No One will ever believe in you or your dreams until they believe that you undoubting believe in yourself and your dreams.

When you foster enough belief in actions. It then becomes second nature and just a natural part of who you are. You will no longer have to proclaim that you are the light, when people can see for themselves the light that shines within and from you without you having to utter even a single word.

Ironically, it's just he same as being a compulsive liar. This person tells so many lies, on top of lies, to cover up lies, until they themselves forget what's the truth and truthfully believe the lie they first told for whatever reason is now the truth. What's more intriguing is, they fight even harder proclaiming their truth, than they did when their truth was still a lie, because they actually believe in themselves for speaking the truth.

Somewhat confusing right? Let's see if I can break it down even more to help us understand.

Before I became the writer the world knows as Sean Ingram, I was just a poor troubled kid named Demont Sean Ingram, who was just getting some anger out of his head and heart by jotting down my frustrations with my life and the world on paper. I never imagined being an author or doing book signings. I was just a poor troubled kid, so why would anyone want to read what I wrote and have my autograph.

As God guided me on this path, I began to grow into the belief that maybe I would be good at this writing thing. Day by day, God would put people in my life to help teach and inspire me to become a writer. My mindset was slowly shifting from seeing myself as that poor troubled kid with nothing of importance to say, but to the young kid that was finding his gift at writing.

Remember when I told you about my teacher/ god mom, Ms. Sutton? Well during my 10th grade year at Greene Central High School, she entered one of my poems into a national poetry contest.

Poets from all across the country, young and old, entered poems with hopes of winning a prized spot into the publisher's anthology called "Poetic Voices of America".

The first place winner would have their poem printed on page 1 of the anthology, and so on and so on. Within the 200-page book, my poem was chosen to appear on page 61. Imagine that. This poor troubled black from down a dirt path in Greene County, NC had been published in a National Poetry Book at the age of 16.

The Anthology validated me now actually being a published writer. My mindset then again shifted. I begin to think of myself as a writer, because I now had proof that I really was.

I began writing more and more. Studying other authors. Studying the dictionary to increase my vocabulary. I thought about different combinations of how I could put words together in my mind, seemingly every second I was awake.

Fast-forwarding five years, I published my first book and 19 years old. I was now an author. Two years later, because of others now seeing me as an author, I started hanging with other authors and met the likes of my close friend and mentor, Omar Tyree.

When I had first published my book, as a new young author, I just wanted the opportunity to meet Omar Tyree and shake his hand, never imagining that even twenty years later, I would have worked with him on numerous projects and have the opportunity to act in and direct his first major stage play he had written.

Trust Me, Dreams Do Come True when you wake up and start living the dream.

I once wrote in a poem, " Who would have thought that when I was in the back of the class sleeping, that I would one day be standing in front of a class teaching. Standing on the same stars that I was once reaching, with thoughts so profound that some even proclaim that I be preaching."

Through the years, I became my belief and manifested my ministry.

"I'm Not Attempting

To Shine On You,

But It Is My Intention

To Show You The Light"

Lesson

"Manifest your Ministry"

MANIFEST
Clearly apparent to sight or understanding; obvious:
1. To show or demonstrate plainly; reveal:
2. To be evidence of; prove:

MINISTRATION
1. The act or process of serving or aiding
2. The act of performing the duties of a minister of religion; to serve:

(Defined by The American Heritage Dictionary of the English Language)

The ministry has always been inside of me, but the reason to release it or share it with the world was something that came far later on in life. If indeed, Ministry, or to Minister, in essence, truthfully means only to spread the good news, then we all have a ministry inside of us.

The question that may be relevant to this matter is, What good news do I have, and if I do have good news of Gods grace and mercy that I can share, am I strong enough to do so without fear of public persecution, and do I have the communication skills to do so that will be understood and respected by anyone?

I often questioned myself, Who Am I to inspire anyone? Who Am I to motivate anyone? What is good about my life that someone else would find pleasure in hearing?

In prison, I learned to Manifest My Ministry. I discovered that despite the negative I had endured, the good news was that I had actually persevered. One day while in a conversation with a young brother on the yard, he asked me questions of how I dealt with and overcame certain situations in my life. In his eyes, I was strong and knowledgeable because of the image he saw me as a well-known poet and spoken word artist on the yard. I shared with him my truth, unknowingly; my truth would also be a reality that he could all to well relate to.

My story of perseverance inspired him that he could do the same also. That conversation with him allowed me to reflect over my career as an author and spoken word artist. I thought about all of the times I stood on a stage confused, wondering why as I cry my soul out on stage through my spoken word lyrics of my heartache and pain, people would smile and more often than not, applaud in standing ovation. It truly confused me until I began to grow into the understanding of my gift.

Truth is, many applauded the fact that I said publicly what they have always felt, but was afraid to say, so in essence I became the un-official voice of the voiceless.

They could relate and appreciate my truth because my truth was also theirs, or even someone else they knew. When I spoke about my childhood, it reminded them of theirs. When I spoke of the love of my grandmother, it allowed them to see the face of their grandmother.

When I spoke of my secret emotions of fear, loneliness and despondency, it allowed them to relate and connect with me on a deeper and more personal level, because they have also at some point felt those same emotions. When I cried on stage though my lyrics, I cried for them also. When I spoke of the victory of persevering and overcoming those obstacles in life, I championed their fight also.

I then began to appreciate their appreciation of me, which also changed my mindset, perspective and appreciation of my gift.

One day during a performance on the rec-yard before over twenty-five hundred inmates at Butner Federal Prison. I spoke from the bottom of my soul to inspire my incarcerated brothers that the sun would one day in time shine our way again. I spoke as I never spoke before.

The crowed feel silent. I looked over the crowed to see a sea of faces, blacks, whites, mexicans, and all others in between and abroad looking on directly at me. No one uttered a word, guys even stopped running the track and working out. I could feel the energy building up inside of me as if I was a volcano preparing to erupt. I finished my poem and the inmates erupted in applause and cheer. It truly baffled me, because in a situation of circumstance such as being incarcerated in prison, I would have never imagined to have inspired, motivated or even brought joy to guys that have been locked up, or will remain locked up for years on end. It was a revelation of the confirmation of the conversation I had with God when I was in solitary confinement.

When I walked off the stage, guys stood in anticipation to shake my hand and inform me that the poem I had spoke was meant just for them for that very moment. It made me feel good to know that despite our current situation, for those three to five minutes, I was able to make them feel good, I was able to inspire them and mentally free their mind from the prison we all were physically bound within.

My big homie Ron G even told me how I was a breathe of fresh air in a fiery furnace. Big Rob even made me promise him that I would never forsake my mission in life. I thought to myself that Saul Williams had done it in the movie "SLAM", but I was actually doing it in real life. It made me realize that if I had the gift and power to inspire brothers in a situation such as we were in, then how could I not have the gift to inspire the world. I silently assured God that I was ready to take the challenge of his mission and ministry, and from that moment on, I have attacked the crafting of my gift with a new purpose.

Introduced to a new perspective of my gift of writing and communicating, I began to study day in and day out to hone my craft. I began to read and write daily rather than when I just wanted to or when I would be come inspired to do so. I began studying the dictionary in order to increase my vocabulary, as well as my knowledge of the meaning of words.

I figured that for me to become a great writer, I was to also become a wordsmith. I began to read books for the purpose to study the author. I then began to understand the difference between the many different styles of writing I came across, such the essence of great storytellers such as Donald Goins and Dan Brown.

Daily I thought of different ways to enhance my gifts to manifest my ministry. I began to study sociology and phycology to better understand the mindset of different people dividing my research by race, economic and social status and educational levels so I could relate to people across the board. I desired to captivate, intrigue, empower and tap into the emotional realm of each person that would hear my voice or read my words. I began to study the mindset of people like I never studied before. I began to learn how to decipher and comprehend different conversations, which allowed me to expand the range of people I would begin to communicate with.

Without knowing, I had the personality that would allow me to cross bridges that many of my status and background wouldn't be allowed to have the pleasure to cross. Being that I had this opportunity, I felt obligated to be the spokesperson of all of those who come from where I come, those who have traveled my same path in life, those who many proclaimed they would never achieve because they was thought of as the less than. I dedicated myself to being the voice of the voiceless.

Establishing anything of great substance and value is a slow process. It's similar to building a house from the ground up. Most people just move in without second thought of the process it took for them to actually live in and enjoy their dream house.

But what if by chance, the owner of the house themselves cleared the land, formed the foundation, built the frame, installed all of the electrical, plumbing, air conditioning and sheet rock for the walls. Imagined if the owner painted their entire house themselves with every color they previously envisioned within their dreams while dreaming of their dream house. Imagine the different level of respect and appreciation the owner would have for their dream house, rather than if they just discovered it online and simply had the opportunity to afford to purchase the house.

Establishing, or Manifesting your Ministry is in essence the same. Every trial and tribulation that you have ever endured, every heartache you have ever felt, every moment of loneliness and depression that you have been subjected to have been test for you to pass, as well as, for you to past, in order to enhance your testimony. Your experience in life will solidify you as an expert within the message of your ministry.

I found as I continued to grow as a spoken word artist that my truth was my ministry, and the stage was my pulpit.

I now began to understand the conversation I had with God more and more concerning me "spreading the good news".

I realized that my way of spreading the good news of how God saved me was through my spoken word. My way to teach about Gods grace and mercy was through my spoken word. Through my words and voice in spoken word, I became a minister, and my ministry is to spread the good news of God within my poems, short stories, stage plays, spoken word performances, and motivational speeches.

"Are You Waiting

On Your Success,

Or Is Your Success

Waiting On You?"

Lesson 14

"Invent your Importance"

INVENT

Create or design (something that has not existed before); be the originator of.
1. Make up (an idea, name, story, etc.), especially so as to deceive.

IMPORTANCE

The state or fact of being a great significance or value.

(Defined by The American Heritage Dictionary of the English Language)

When there is no opportunity, create one. My life began to change when my attitude and mindset changed. I stopped asking for opportunities and started offering opportunities.

I began to no longer ask for handouts, but yet, look for ways and opportunities I could offer a helping hand.

You will hear me proclaim over and over again until the end of my days that the game of life is not that of checkers, but yet of chess. Positioning must be purposeful. Each move must be masterful. The beginning must be played with end in mind.

I created my mentoring and creative writing programs because I saw the need for it and understand the importance of being able to articulate thoughts and ideas. I understand that in life we are at competition with each other for every job opportunity, woman or man we want to win the heart of, and every position we desire to stand in.

I am a writer in my mind, heart and soul. I'm a very good writer at that. Within in my own struggles writing, I created a writing process that helped me tremendously. Knowing how much it helped me, I was positive that it would help others also.

I introduced my programs to the schools and community college, and offered the opportunity for me to come in and teach my writing their students in order to help their students, which would ultimately increase grade scores.

I also offered my gift to inspire uninspired students to learn. I offered my services of being a mentor. I knew what I needed when I was their age, but often didn't have.

I invented my importance by helping at-risk-youth see and find the light I had so often for and finally found in prison. I thought; if I could save them from falling into the hole of prison, let me shine the light on them so they can see the hole in the dark.

I'm no different from our youth today. When I look at them, I see myself. I teach them what somebody did, or what I wish someone had taught me. I say to them to inspire what someone said, or I wish someone had said to me.

When asked that familiar question. "Why Me?" now my answer stays the same but even stronger, "Why Not Me, and who better than me?"

As a creator, it is my mission to create. Truly believing now in my creative ability, I think first to create my opportunities rather than now searching for opportunities. I guess you can say as I did, that I believed it until I became it.

Currently I work with the Wake County Juvenile System, providing a juvenile diversion program through The Sean Ingram Academy. I focus on Character Development as the foundation of my teachings to our youth. I truly believe that if I can change their mindset for the better, then I can change their outcome in life to be for the better.

Once in a meeting with the Juvenile Crime Prevention Council, I was questioned about my program and my reason for focusing on Character Development as my foundation. In short, they wanted to know what proof did I have that Character Development was an evidence-based program and what evidence did I have.

I replied humbly as possible, "Yes, and I, Sean Ingram is your evidence". I continued to explain the fact that an alcoholic don't quit drinking because they don't like the taste of their favorite liquor anymore, but yet, because the doctor told them that's it harming or killing them, and if they want to live, they must make the choice to stop drinking. Their wanting of positive outweighed their curiosity for negative.

"The Man Who Is

Serenely Silent,

Intimidates Me More

Than The Man

Who Constantly Screams"

Lesson 15

"Understand your Uniqueness"

UNDERSTAND

Perceive the intended meaning of (words, a language, or speaker).

1. Infer something from information received (often used as a polite formula in conversation).

UNIQUENESS

The quality of being the only one of its kind.

2. The quality of being particularly remarkable, special, or unusual.

(Defined by The American Heritage Dictionary of the English Language)

I ask myself, just as I will ask you. What makes you different from everybody else and what makes you stand out within the masses.

Listening to music these days really makes me realize how important it is to be original and unique. If ten different rap songs play on the radio, I will probably think it's the same rapper with just a slight different beat. Singers, the same. I hear very little originality in music that allows me to distinguish between the different apart from each other.

Same rhythm, same tempo, same bounce, same thoughts. What's different?

The original print of a picture will always be much more superb in color and quality than the copy of the original. In fact, every time the copy is copied, the color and quality decreases more and more each time until the original is barely even recognizable anymore.

I contribute this epidemic to the lack of creativity of our youth and work ethic. I'm starting to notice the ongoing pattern of it being cool to be a copycat. Being a copycat was a big No No in my days, but someway has become cool and the norm.

Most young artist of today just hear or see something and say, "That's Hot, I'm gonna do that". Then a new song and style come out and they the same thing, "Did you hear that new Drake song?, that's hot, I'm gonna do that!".

I guess they want the hit song, and all of the fame and fortune that comes with having a hit song, but don't want to go through the process that it sometimes take for that hit song. The years of thinking and putting together combinations that don't match sometimes to create that hit song.

Longevity comes from Originality. Understand your Uniqueness and build a foundation of your own that will keep your empire standing forever.

"Being Dumb

Is a Condition,

But Being Stupid

Is a State Of Mind"

Lesson 16

"Prioritize your Passion"

PRIORITIZE

Designate or treat (something) as more important than other things.
1. Determine the order for dealing with (a series of items or task) according to their relative importance.

PASSION

A strong and barely controllable emotion.

(Defined by The American Heritage Dictionary of the English Language)

I must admit that for the majority of my career, life for that matter, I did not or know how to prioritize my passion.

I would also always find myself being distracted from the projects I had been working on, or the things I had going on in my life, in order to help others. I have always been a person who desired to help and save others on a sinking ship, even while my own ship is sinking as well.

It was imperative that I learned to say no and over extend my already overwhelmed self. In the words of my dear friend and poetic brother, Life @LifeSpeaksLife, I had to learn that if it doesn't Evolve Me, then it shouldn't Involve Me.

By no means saying we shouldn't help people in life, but I am saying that you have to put yourself in a position to be able to truly help first. Simple mathematics teaches us that we can't give what we don't have.

Please understand, I'm speaking on a larger scale than that of just finances, but that of time and energy. Time and Energy is the greatest commodity you will ever have the opportunity in life to possess.

Time and Energy is a million times more valuable than any one dollar you can put in your pocket.

Today I can make fifty dollars. Tomorrow I can lose a hundred dollars. The very next day if I play my cards right, I can gain back the hundred I lost and still maybe go up another two hundred dollars.

Time and Energy is totally different and you can't afford to gamble with it as we often think we can. Once Time and Energy is lost, it's gone forever. More often than not, the same applies to Opportunities. Once an opportunity is lost, it's a slim to none chance that the opportunity will re-present itself.

It is absolutely true that another will come in it's place, but the question is, will you be ready to optimize that new opportunity, or will you let it pass you just as the others because you wasn't ready to catch because you was looking in the stands at a familiar face while the ball was coming down the third base line.

I once heard, true or not, that in life, people will only get two great opportunities in life. It was said that the first great opportunity comes we are to young to recognize it, therefor it passes us without a second look. The second great opportunity comes later in life you need it the most, but will you be ready for it.

As a writer, spoken word artist, and now as a motivational speaker my days are spent working on my craft. Preparing myself in advance for my next opportunity.

My priority in life now is being prepared. The last minute phone call to speak or perform no longer intimidates me, because I've been preparing for moments like this my entire career.

My grandma use to say that if you stay ready, then you don't have to get ready.

Prioritize your Passion and be ready when your opportunity comes. When friends want to hang out, but you have that test, that game, or that class the next day you have to be prepared for in order to win and succeed, just remember to put your priorities in order.

"I Know I Will

Die On (a) Tomorrow,

But I Question

Have I Truly Lived

On (a) Today"

Lesson

"Prophesize your Purpose"

PROPHESIZE
To utter prophecies
1. To predict or foretell.

PURPOSE
The reason for which something is done or created
1. For which something exists.
2. To have as one's intention or objective.

(Defined by The American Heritage Dictionary of the English Language)

I told them that I would be,

but they didn't believe, and still don't,

even though they have the proof to see

I proclaimed,

even while they screamed me to be liar

it confused me, and I couldn't stoop to their level

because my thoughts was just that much higher

I was born to be

or rather God sent me

to write a new story for children

who also came from nothing

Imagine that, because of me

they now believe in the possibility

of what can miraculously be

They diagnosed me as crazy

because I believed in what they couldn't see

I never claimed to be Jesus

but I am just as confident as he in Gods plan for me

My purpose is to inspire

My ministry is to motivate

And with my words

I elevate

I know they can't understand

Cause they can only see the flesh

Of this spiritual man

"I Am Sean Ingram

Because He Is God"

Lesson 18

"Define your Devotion"

DEFINE
The act of defining or making something definite, distinct, or clear.

DEVOTION
1. Love, loyalty, or enthusiasm for a person, activity, or particular cause.
2. The act of performing the duties of a minister of religion; to serve:

(Defined by The American Heritage Dictionary of the English Language)

While in prison, I was once asked if I was a "Religious Goffer", meaning was I one who was gonna for this or that when it was convenient for me, or because someone else I knew was involved with it. I guess my religious integrity and alliance was being questioned.

My uncle, Wade Best, worshiped with the Nation of Islam. I had other friends who worshiped as Sunni Muslims, Christians, and some even in the Moorish Science Temple of America.

I never thought of myself as being a goffer as they would call it, but just a brother who respected my brothers and their beliefs, be it the same or different from mine.

I enjoyed fellowshipping with my brothers, regardless of the religious preference. I'm not for separation, but finding a common thread we can bond our relationship with.

I stay true to my truth and stand for what is righteous. If a Muslim baby is crying from hunger, should I not feed that baby because he or she is not Christian?

Unfortunately, America is built on the foundation of separation when it comes to race and religion. I encourage you to not put yourself in a box that society has secretly awaiting for you as a fox trap.

Don't leave it up to chance for other people to define your beliefs, religious or personal. Be your own voice and have no reservations about you being you, whether accepted by others or not.

Never allow the bright shimmer of fools' gold to distract you or blind you from seeing what truly matters in your life. Stay devoted to those who have been devoted to you throughout your entire process from the struggle to success.

Be careful of those who will always have ideas of what you need to be doing, but aren't doing it for themselves or has never done what you are doing.

Remember, leaders lead by example, therefore whoever you choose to follow as a mentor, make sure they are taking you in the direction you need to be going. If see that the car is detouring to another route that is taking you off course, then quickly stop the car and get out, even if you have to walk to begin to find the course you need to get back on.

"If You Don't Put Forth

Any Efforts In Today,

Then What Expectations

Can You Have

From Tomorrow"

Lesson

"Perfect your Presentation"

PERFECT

Having all the required or desirable elements, qualities, or characteristics, as good as it can possibly to be.

1. Absolute, or complete.

PRESENTATION

The way in which something is presented.

1. An activity in which someone shows, describes, or explains something to a group of people.

(Defined by The American Heritage Dictionary of the English Language)

I know there are eyes looking at me constantly. Some look at me from a far. Some look at me in passing wondering if I am indeed, him. Some look at me in observation when the time presents itself that we are in the same space and time. Others look at me with a critical eye online, be it my websites or my many other social media outlets.

I can no longer hide. There is no rock for me to hide under to escape the criticism of the world. I am an open target to every opinion of Sean Ingram, be it good or bad.

My friend, mentor, and professional etiquette and protocol coach, Mr. Floyed Chavis, always remind me that I have to be aware of my presentation at all times. Unfortunately, there are no off times for public figures.

Mr. Chavis teaches me that even before I open my mouth, I am being evaluated on just my mere presentation. I'm judged on the way I walk, the way I dress, the way I shake hands, and even the way I eat.

Some days it gets very overwhelming to have people constantly judging and criticizing me. Some times the negative comments posted about me online hurts, especially when all I try to do is the best I can.

It often confuses me when I ponder the thought if people cared this much about well being when I was in prison, or the days I went hungry, or even the nights I had to sleep in my car because I had nowhere else to go at the time.

I guess that no longer matters now, if it ever will again because my stage lights are on, the curtains are open, and now all eyes are on me.

Your presentation is your first business card, and speaks more for you than your resume ever will. I also learned in time, that you will never know who is looking on at you. Even when you feel like no one is watching, you can count on it, that someone always has an eye on you.

Your presentation will make or break you in business. As a matter of fact, your presentation will keep you from obtaining a job faster than your lack of education. Many job interviews are ended as soon the potential candidate walks in the door, just based on the presentation alone.

After the initial observation, now it's time to present your thoughts and ideas. Your communication skills dictate your intellect.

Regardless of what your resume may say, employers read you inside and out.

It often hurts me to look at my young brothers and sisters going to job interviews dressed like they are going to a club. I hear them talking to the person they are asking a job from as if they are talking to their friends. Most have no distinction between personal and professional.

I often if some even looked in the mirror before left home, or if they ever give thought that if their presentation would properly represent the company they are applying for a job.

I'm all about freedom of expression, but I also understand there is a time and place for my personal expression.

Being a Spoken Word Artist and Motivational Speaker, I had to learn to perfect my presentation. If I desire to charge $500 for an hour speech, I have to be at least worth $1000. Les Brown taught me to always do more than what's required of me, and my phone will continue to ring.

"It's Impossible

To Love Others

Without First

Loving Yourself"

Lesson 20

"Motivate your Movement"

MOTIVATE

To provide with motive to do something.
1. To stimulate (someone's) interest in or enthusiasm for doing something.

MOVEMENT

1. A group of people working together to advance their shared political, social, or artistic ideas.
2. An act of changing physical location or position or of having this changed.

(Defined by The American Heritage Dictionary of the English Language)

Being that people don't even want to get up to change the channel on their own television, what makes you think they want to put in the effort to go out of their way to do something that you want of them, when they don't even want to do it for something that they want for themselves.

In a world of so much negativity and depression, it's becoming a lot more difficult to gain the support of people, not to mention, financial support, be it in the form of donations or sales.

Now more than ever, people are supporting and buying products based off of their emotions rather than logic of needs. What makes you or your product so special that will motivate people to want it.

Early in my career, I was taught by a publicist to Never Sale A Product, but to Always Sale Myself. She explained that if I sold, Sean Ingram, then no matter what product Sean Ingram offered, the people will support it because they support Sean Ingram, not just a particular book, cd, or stage play.

I found her advice to me very beneficial through my years. I Motivate my Movement by allowing people to be a part of the Sean Ingram Movement. In a sense, I allow others a chance others to buy a ticket to ride on the Sean Ingram bandwagon. My bandwagon is like a party bus that is riding towards the finish line of success. The songs playing are filled with inspirational words, good vibes, and a band of musicians that will energize their despondent soul.

With their all-inclusive ticket, not only do they get to take the ride towards my success, but they also get to catch a ride to their own destination of success.

My method stays simple. I support those who support me. Understanding, as my brother Dj Damu explained, that your network will determine your net-worth, I make it clear and understood the return they can expect from investing in me, and that investing in me is also indirectly investing into themselves, their youth, and their community.

"Others Will Never

Believe In You,

Unless They Can

Truly Believe That

You Believe In Yourself"

Lesson 21

"Stimulate your Support"

STIMULATE
Encourage interest or activity
1. Encourage development of or increased activity in
(a state or process).

SUPPORT
Give assistance to, especially financially
2. Enable to function or act.

(Defined by The American Heritage Dictionary of the English Language)

Once you have accomplished the task of motivating the masses to join your movement, the next step is to stimulate their support.

Lets use church as an example. We have motivated them to come to church, so now we at least have them in the door.

During the service is where the stimulation begins. The music, the singing, the prayers, and the message all bring about the stimulation.

This stimulation creates a certain energy that can't be denied or contained. Most often it is described as The Holy Ghost moving through the church, causing people to stand up and shout because the energy they're feeling begins to overwhelm them.

Once the energy is at its peak, then the collection plate comes around and people are more than ready and willing to support.

In business, we have to create that same stimulation. I realized that when I speak or perform at my max, I sell more books and t-shirts. The same can be said about when my energy levels are low or if I'm sick and I'm only performing about 70%, my product sales reflect my performance.

Jay Z said it best, "I'm not a businessman, I'm a business, man". Ironically, this is the mindset that most will never understand.

It's just a the publicist explained to me years and years ago, the reason I should never sale a product, but always sale myself, which is the brand of Sean Ingram.

While building the foundation for The Sean Ingram, I was forced to take a major step back in order to move forward in a new direction.

I started out marketing and branding my academy, but soon realized that I was going away from my original strategy that I had built my career on. I took a step back to begin again my method of CEO BRANDING. I had to get back to marketing Sean Ingram, which would indirectly market my Academy, my Speeches, my Books, my CD's, my Clothing Collection, and every other adventure I dared to take.

I noticed that my supporters truly support all of things I do, because they support me.

*"**Would You**

Still Play The Game,

If God Was Saying It

Instead of Simon?"*

Lesson 22

"Justify your Journey"

JUSTIFY
Show or prove to be right or reasonable.

JOURNEY
An act of traveling from one place to another.

(Defined by The American Heritage Dictionary of the English Language)

In my case, my journey from poverty, to prison, to prosperity has been one hell of a life full of struggle and sacrifice. Since my childhood, all I've ever known is heartache and pain. Everyday brought a different fight. Day after Day, Fight after Fight, I had to learn to smile through it all, even in the face of adversity.

I think back on the many days I wanted to give up and commit suicide. I think about the times my thoughts feel into the abyss of depression and it sometimes took me weeks to find my way out.

I reminisce on the many tears I wanted to cry, but didn't know how. I think back over the moments I hated the reflection I saw in the mirror, because I never learned to love myself.

Despite it all, I can now thank God for every second of my life, because I know understand that it has all been for the good of Gods mission for me.

I've learned to Justify my Journey by realizing the importance of me persevering my process. It all works hand and hand for Gods purpose for you.

No matter what situations you may go through. Despite the turmoil you will have to endure. Look, Listen and Learn from each situation and Thank God for yet again bringing you through another circumstance that seemed beyond your control.

Because of my dark past, I can now see my bright future. Because of my heartache, I can now help mend broken hearts.

Because of my time in prison, I can now help detour our youth from falling into the same hole of destruction.

If I had never gone through any of things, I have no doubt that I would still be successful, but I'm sure I wouldn't be the author, spoken word artist, and the motivational speaker the world knows as, Sean Ingram.

"The Light House

Continues To Shine,

Even When

You Can't See It"

Lesson

"Optimize your Opportunity"

OPTIMIZE

Make the best or most effective use of (a situation, opportunity, or resource).

OPPORTUNITY

A set of circumstances that makes it possible to do something.

1. A chance for employment or promotion.

(Defined by The American Heritage Dictionary of the English Language)

Opportunities may not present itself everyday, and will most likely come when you least expect. You will never meet anyone else in this world that is busier than opportunity.

When opportunity calls or knocks on your door, you have to be ready to go right then, because unfortunately, opportunity will unlikely wait for you to get ready before it starts calling on the next person on its list.

I told you the story when "I couldn't afford to go, but couldn't afford NOT to go even more".

Opportunity may even be wearing a disguise, not allowing you to see it in plain view. You may be looking for a certain person who you think is holding your key to open the door of opportunity, but in fact, you soon realize that the person who is holding your key is that kid you helped with a math test during a tutoring workshop you're involved with at your school to receive your community service credits.

Unknowing to you, this kid is the son of the gentleman you want to meet for a job.

It is my mindset to speak and perform every time as if it's my last, because I never know who's the one person out of the twenty-five sitting in the audience that will be the very person to provide that next opportunity that will help me advance my career and possibly change my life for the better.

When you do get a chance to take advantage of an opportunity, don't just do a good job, do a great job. Doing a great job attracts other opportunities. It's simply another aspect of The Law of Attraction.

Optimize every Opportunity. Connecting opportunities is the same a connecting the dots to a beautiful picture. With each line from dot to dot, opportunity to opportunity, you are getting one step closer to your finish line of success.

"Just Because

Favor Isn't Fair

Doesn't Mean

That I Don't Deserve It"

Lesson 24

"Validate your Value"

VALIDATE

Check or prove the validity or accuracy of (something).
1. Make or declare legally valid.

VALUE

The regard that something is held to deserve.
1. The importance, worth, or usefulness of something.
2. Considered to be beneficial.

(Defined by The American Heritage Dictionary of the English Language)

Les Brown told me to always do more than what's required of me. Example; If you're charging $10 for your work, then let the work you are doing be worth at least $15 or $20.

Going back to the concept of simple, third grade mathematics. You can't expect the reward of a 100% return if you only put in the effort of 20% investment.

Be worth more than you ask for and what in turn will happen, instead of you making the phone calls looking for work, your phone will start ringing from people calling you seeking out your services.

Create your demand. Once you become a demand, now you can create and dictate your price range. Validate your value by knowing that you are worth every penny you ask for and more.

Understanding assets is a very important key to this process, and understanding that you are an asset is even more imperative.

It took me twenty years to build my name and brand. Every day for twenty years, hour-by-hour, I have worked towards reaching a finishing that I had only heard of, but had no sight of it at all.

I paid to perform at poetry open mics many many years before I even received my first invitation to be a feature. After finding myself on the level of being considered as featured artist, and no longer just an open mic participant, I still didn't see and pay for featuring. I created my books to generate income in order for me to optimize my opportunity for being a feature.

Years later, I found myself continuing to rise in the levels of being a featured spoken word artist, and now I was being offered $25 or $50. As my name and brand increased, the amount of my pay increased also, to the point I can comfortably require $500 for each spoken word performance.

I have invested years and years of studying and perfecting my craft, therefore there is no doubt in my mind that I'm worth every dollar I require.

Without Doubt, I am assured that I am asset to myself and others. I'm now more than confident that I am deserving of any success that I have and will obtain in the future.

"The Worlds

Perception Of You

Will Only Be

What You Allow The To See"

Lesson 25

"Brand your Business"

BRAND
An identifying mark used to distinguish from others.

BUSINESS
1. The practice of making one's living by engaging in commerce.
2. A person's regular occupation, profession, or trade.

(Defined by The American Heritage Dictionary of the English Language)

Remember: You are Your Business. You represent how the world will view and judge your business. Based off of their judgments, comes the determination if they will indeed support you or your business.

Also Note, there is a difference between marketing and branding. The Big Mac is a popular sandwich that is marketed by McDonalds, but McDonalds is the Brand in which the foundation of the company was built upon.

Regardless if the Big Mac never sales again, it will just get discontinued and replaced with another burger to be marketed to make up for the profit loss of the Big Mac, but losing the Big Mac will never force McDonalds to shut down and close its doors.

Sean Ingram & Company and The Sean Ingram Academy are my companies, but Sean Ingram is my Brand. Every book I write falls under the brand of Sean Ingram. Every stage play I act in is promoted by power of the Sean Ingram brand.

The Sean Ingram Clothing Collection is made of the same cloth material as Ralph Lauren Polo Shirts, but what makes the major difference in the price is the level of the brand.

Truthfully, people don't pay for the product, but yet, they pay for the brand. That's what makes the difference between buying a water bottle from the Dollar Store as to Macey's. Both product are plastic, even the same color. Both hold water that you drink from. The only difference sometimes is the name or brand on the bottle.

Build your Brand on a solid foundation that will support your empire forever. Brand your Business with the mindset of Quality over Quantity.

Let Longevity be your long-term goal in business. Don't focus on the money, because in time, the money will surely come if you build your business in a manner that will stand the test of time.

Steve Jobs didn't start Apple Computers in Silicon Valley hundreds of acres of land, but rather in his little dirty garage at his parent's house. The same goes with Chick-Fila, McDonalds and many of the other great brands we are familiar with today.

Walt Disney was just a country boy who liked to draw. During his process to success, he went broke, became homeless, lost friends, but he never lost sight of his dreams and he never gave up.

Walt even had to eat out of trash cans at times, and within his lowest times was birth his greatest idea of Mickey Mouse, the very mouse he use to feed while eating out of trash cans himself.

Imagine that, and now the brand of The Walt Disney Company has a net worth of over 85 Billion Dollars.

Steve Jobs, a guy who went broke and fired from the very company he created, in time, through the many ups and downs in his career built Apple Computers brand to have a net worth of over 1.4 Trillion Dollars as of to date.

Conclusion:

"The Devil is a Liar, God is The Truth, and I Am the Proof"

"Testify your Triumph"

TESTIFY
Serve as evidence or proof of something existing.

TRIUMPH
A great victory or achievement.

(Defined by The American Heritage Dictionary of the English Language)

Testify your Triumph and Spread The Good News of Gods Grace and Mercy. This is your Ministry!

Be a beacon of light to others who may still be traveling in darkness. No Matter what point you are in life, we can always share a word of advice to help someone get from point A to B, if indeed we have already ourselves made it to point C. Our Goal is Z.

I will never attempt to shine on my people, but it is my desire to show everyone the light...

God Bless You All!

Sean Ingram is also the author of...

Tears of an Empty Pen
Poetic Prayers of a Fallen Angel
The Passion of the Pen
The Soul of Saratoga Slim

Sean Ingram's
Top 10 Rules for Success

1. Believe in God, and the reason he desired you to be.

2. Trust and Believe in yourself, and your vision.

3. Recognize your reason, do what you love to do, and be passionate about it.

4. Persevere your process, and never give up.

5. Only compete with yourself, and your own capabilities.

6. Stay true to your truth.

7. Be confident in your convictions.

8. Remain humble and hungry.

9. Stay emotionally connected to your dreams and goals.

10. Never allow your ignorance to eclipse your intellect.

#SeanIngramSpeaks
Success is not about what you can do, but yet, it's about what you can endure.

www.SeanIngram.info

CPSIA information can be obtained
at www.ICGtesting.com
Printed in the USA
FFOW03n0409170318
45664409-46487FF